Tradition » Passion » Perfection

Giles Fallowfield is an acknowledged expert on champagne. He is the consultant on champagne for Oz Clarke's *Pocket Wine Book* and a regular contributor to *Imbibe* and *Square Meal* magazines. His work also appears in *Drinks International, Decanter, The Drinks Business,* and *The Daily Telegraph.* He won the Lanson "Champagne Writer of the Year Award" in 2001 and 2003. His website is www.champagneguru.co.uk.

W. Craig Cooper has spent the last twelve years as beverage director and educator at Pops for Champagne in Chicago. Cooper has traveled the Champagne region extensively and has taken it upon himself to demystify this legendary wine for his own understanding and for the enjoyment of his many happy guests.

Princeton Architectural Press
37 East Seventh Street
New York, NY 10003
Visit our website at www.papress.com

Conceived and produced by
Elwin Street Productions
3 Percy Street
London W1T 1DE
www.elwinstreet.com

Illustrations: Tonwen Jones
Picture credits: Champagne Marguet Père & Fils: p. 115;
Collection CIVC: pp. 18 (Michel Guillard), 76 (Visuel Impact),
90 (Michel Guillard), 115 (Divers); Photolibrary.com: p. 44

Recipes supplied by: St Pancras Grand Champagne Bar
(Blushing Bubbles and French 75), Texture Bar (Luxury
Mojito), and Pops for Champagne (La Vie en Rose)

Library of Congress Cataloging-in-Publication Data
Fallowfield, Giles.
Champagne / Giles Fallowfield and W. Craig Cooper. —
First edition.
pages cm — (Instant expert : tradition, passion,
perfection)
Includes index.
ISBN 978-1-61689-241-8 (alk. paper)
Champagne (Wine) I. Cooper, W. Craig. II. Title.
TP555.F36 2014
663'.224—dc23
2013027810

CHAMPAGNE

Giles Fallowfield
W. Craig Cooper

Princeton Architectural Press, New York

Contents

Why be an expert of champagne?

Champagne is one of the world's great white wines. It enjoys a unique position as *the* drink of celebration, but today is also increasingly seen as a fine wine with a myriad of different styles. Knowing more about the wines and styles that are available will enhance your appreciation, expand the occasions on which you drink it, and increase your enjoyment when you do.

At its glorious best, champagne—particularly vintage champagne near the peak of its maturity, as some of the best 1996s currently are—can provide a drinking experience without equal: that magical combination of initial freshness with the Burgundy-like wine complexities champagne tends to develop with age.

Although high-quality sparkling wine is made in quite a few different countries, it is widely accepted that the world's most celebrated and sought-after examples all come from within the Champagne appellation in northeast France. No other region regularly turns out sparkling wines of such intensity and complexity that are also long lasting, thanks partly to their high natural acidity.

What is it that makes champagne special and helps to distinguish it from other quality sparkling wines? A simple answer is "cool climate," which lies at the heart of champagne production and in part explains how it originally came to be made. In the early days of winemaking in this cool northerly region, the first alcoholic fermentation would grind to a halt as the temperature dropped with the onset of winter—often before it was complete and the natural yeasts had turned all the sugar in the grapes into alcohol. When spring arrived and the temperatures started to rise, the wines, already in bottle, would start to ferment again, giving them a slight spritz.

While the cool climate partly explains the very existence of champagne, it is also one of the keys to the wine's quality. The Champagne region is France's most northerly vineyard, which makes it the perfect place to produce the thin, acid base wine from which top-quality fizz is made. The relatively high acidity in the grapes, a vital ingredient in champagne's long aging, is naturally preserved by the slow ripening process this far north.

Champagne is able to age slowly and gracefully, adding nuances of flavor and complexity while still retaining a delightful freshness for many years. It is this quality that sets the top level of champagne production apart from even the best sparkling wines made elsewhere around the world.

Of course, champagne is not solely the result of a marginal climate. It is a magical combination of climate, chalky soil, and hundreds of years of human endeavor—refining, adjusting, and improving both vine cultivation and winemaking—that enables something unique to emerge in the bottle.

Not all champagne is great. There are literally thousands of producers, and it is certainly not true that they all achieve the high level of quality that a connoisseur would rightly expect from a bottle of champagne. More than 350 million bottles can be made following a bountiful harvest, and a large chunk of them are sold at the entry-level price of between $30 and $40 per bottle. If you judged champagne by the standard of the product in this price sector, you may wonder what all the fuss is about.

However, there are also a number of houses, cooperatives, and individual growers who make wines that are really worthy of the name champagne. It is the very best of these that are highlighted in the chapters that follow. Typically, each producer makes a number of different champagnes, but it is their most typical and finest products that are featured. Where a champagne is considered of particularly high quality, it has been highlighted as an "Instant Expert Essential."

This is not meant to be an exhaustive list but rather a personal selection drawn from more than two decades of visiting this fascinating region and tasting wines with the men and women who make them. Thanks to the generosity of the Champenois (people from Champagne), I have managed to sample many of the region's finest wines and a wide selection of the top vintages produced there over the past ten decades. I hope you will be able to use the tips and recommendations in this book to find some of your own ultimate champagne drinking experiences.

» Fundamentals

The production regions

The Champagne appellation extends ninety-three miles north to south and nearly seventy-five miles east to west. This is not one continuous stretch of vineyard, but rather various separate groupings, with five main production areas: Montagne de Reims, Vallée de la Marne, Côte des Blancs, Côte de Sézanne, and the Côte des Bar. Although each one is strongly associated with a particular grape, because the soils and aspects are not identical across the region, pockets of all three main grape varieties (see page 13) are found in each.

The 319 villages in the Champagne area are quality-rated under a system known as the *échelle des crus*, literally "ladder of growths," and given a classification between 80 and 100 percent. Of these, 258 are assessed between 80 and 89 percent; forty-four are *premiers crus*, between 90 and 99 percent; and seventeen are *grands crus* villages, rated 100 percent. The latter are all in the three best-known districts, with nine in the Montagne de Reims, six in the Côte des Blancs, and two in the Vallée de la Marne.

Montagne de Reims

This region is best known for black grapes; the reputations of the *grands crus* villages of Mailly, Verzenay, Verzy, Ambonnay, and Bouzy are based on Pinot Noir. It is the most widely planted grape in the region, but there are areas where Pinot Meunier is more evident and important pockets of Chardonnay.

The differing microclimates, aspects, and exposures of individual sites result in a large range of wine styles. The soil types may also vary, although all the *grands crus* villages sit on the chalky bedrock for which Champagne is rightly famous.

Vallée de la Marne

The vineyards of the Vallée de la Marne are located on clayey, marly, and sandy soils with pockets of alluvial river deposits and less chalk evident as you go west from Épernay. The majority of plantings are Pinot Meunier, which, because of its late bud-break and early ripening, is less vulnerable in this frost-prone valley. Meunier has a reputation as Champagne's workhorse grape, being less refined than the other two, but it is widely used by the major houses because its fruitiness and early development help soften their nonvintage blends, making them more approachable when young.

Côte des Blancs

The vineyards in this region are mostly on the purest form of chalky belemnite subsoil, rich in minerals and trace elements. More than 95 percent are planted with Chardonnay, and grapes from the four *grands crus* villages clustered in the center of the Côte—Cramant, Avize, Oger, and Le Mesnil-sur-Oger—are the most sought after and command the highest price. Not only do they help lift any blend they are added to, pure Côte des Blancs Chardonnay grapes from any of these villages can produce wines of great intensity, minerality, and longevity, although they also tend to be somewhat austere in their youth.

Côte de Sézanne

The subsoil here is mostly clay and clayey silt with pockets of chalk. Like the Côte des Blancs, it is mainly planted with Chardonnay but around one-fifth is given over to Pinot Meunier. Thanks partly to the favorable southeasterly aspect, the wines tend to get riper and be more forward and fruitier than those in the Côte des Blancs; they are also slightly more rustic. The area is rated 87 percent for white grapes and 85 percent for black grapes on the *échelle des crus*.

Côte des Bar

Eighty-three percent of the area is planted with Pinot Noir. In fact, half the appellation's Pinot Noir is planted in the Côte des Bar—the only place in France where wine may be produced under three different appellations: Champagne, Rosé des Riceys, and Coteaux Champenois.

Rare grape varieties

In addition to the three main grapes used to make champagne there are also about 250 acres devoted to four other varieties: Arbanne, Petit Meslier, Pinot Blanc, and Pinot Gris. The latter two you might find elsewhere in Alsace or the New World, but Petit Meslier and Arbanne are rarer, old Champagne varieties most often found in the Côte des Bar. Between them they make up less than 1 percent of grapes planted. Traditionally, those grapes were harder to grow in the region, and so the main three came to dominate the vineyards.

Types of grape

There are several types of grape planted in the region, but there are three main varieties used for champagne, which account for just under 100 percent of grapes planted—about 83,650 acres in total.

Chardonnay

When the grapes are young, expect fresh, lifted citrus notes, plenty of crisp acidity, and some floral aromas. Pure Côte des Blancs Chardonnay can have a flinty, mineral, chalky, even iodine, note on the palate, and a salty hint of the sea.

Pinot Noir

This grape variety brings more body, roundness, and richness to a blend as well as structure. Pinot Noir from the north-facing Montagne de Reims *grands crus* often has a penetrating acidity, which makes it very long-lived.

Pinot Meunier

Often overtly fruity, the grapes may have a slightly rustic note and some spiciness. Blends that use a high percentage of Meunier tend to develop more quickly. They are rarely used to produce a single-varietal champagne, though good examples most certainly exist.

Styles of champagne

All champagne is designated either "vintage" or "nonvintage," but within these two parameters there are many variants of dryness, sweetness, style, quality, and color. The vast majority (at least four out of every five bottles of champagne sold) are classified a brut nonvintage. The "brut" part relates to the amount of residual sugar in the wine (the dosage levels) and can be anything between 0 to 15 grams per liter (g/l) but is typically between 10 and 12 grams.

The level of dosage in brut styles has gradually been coming down, following a decade or so of higher summer temperatures and longer sunshine hours, resulting in riper fruit. Average potential alcohol levels are up, too. Stylistically, there has also been growing

Dosage levels in champagne

Level	Grams per liter
Brut Nature (or Zéro dosage)	0–2
Extra Brut	0–6
Brut	0–15
Extra Sec	12–20
Sec	17–35
Demi-sec	33–50
Doux	50+

interest in bone-dry "extra brut" styles and *non-dosé* champagnes, which have no sugar added at all when they are disgorged.

Nonvintage and vintage champagne

Nonvintage champagne is a blend of two or more harvests. Multivintage might be a better description, as these wines are typically made from one harvest-year base plus reserve wine (see page 76) from two or more previous harvests (see "Blending" on page 20).

Vintage champagne must be made 100 percent from the year indicated on the label. It represents less than 5 percent of champagne produced and is generally produced only in years when the climate is particularly kind. Vintages are widely declared by a majority of producers perhaps three or four times a decade, but these are not necessarily evenly spaced out. For example, at the end of the 1980s, there were three high-class harvests one after another, in 1988, 1989, and 1990. There was then a gap until the classic 1995 vintage, which was immediately followed by another great, but entirely different, style of vintage in 1996.

Blanc de Blancs

A Blanc de Blancs champagne is made entirely from white grapes. The vast majority will be all-Chardonnay, although there are other varieties, including Pinot Blanc, Arbane, and Petit Meslier. A Blanc de Blancs style, especially one made from the *grands crus* villages of the Côte des Blancs, such as Avize or Le Mesnil-sur-Oger, may possess great aging potential. When youthful, the style tends to be unforthcoming and is often quite austere, but it can develop toasty richness -with age.

Blanc de Noirs

Literally "white wine made from black grapes," blanc de noirs in the case of champagne is made from either Pinot Noir or Pinot Meunier, or a blend of the two. It tends to be a richer, fuller style of wine, but good examples are not easy to find, partly because few of the large houses make it. Two good producers that do are merchant house Drappier and grower Serge Mathieu, both of which are based in the Côte des Bar, where Pinot Noir is widely planted.

Rosé

Nearly all pink champagne is made by blending in a little red wine (between 5 and 20 percent), which has also been produced in Champagne, with white champagne—the more red wine you use, the darker the hue of the rosé. In Europe, this method of making a rosé wine is allowed only within the Champagne appellation. Pink fizz may also be made by the *saignée* method, in which pigment to color the wine is bled from the skins (most rosé table wine is made like this), but few producers use this method, partly because it is more difficult to do and to control the resulting color; one house that does is Laurent-Perrier. Some smaller producers these days use a combination of the two methods.

Rosé champagne has been the fastest growing sector of the champagne market since the millennium, partly because better, softer, and fruitier styles are now being made more widely. Unvintaged rosé champagne is invariably more expensive than its white counterparts and is often priced at a similar level to vintage champagne.

Prestige Cuvée

Most producers, large and small, make a wine that they would put in this category. Typically at the top of the range, the most expensive, and often specially packaged, this will be their effort to produce the best, most impressive champagne from the grapes they have access to. In some respects this sector is defined by champagne's icon brands—Dom Pérignon, Cristal, and Krug—but other top producers make wines of similar quality and complexity.

Single-vineyard wines

Most champagne is made by blending together grapes from different vineyards (see page 20), but in recent years interest has grown in wines made from grapes picked on individual sites that have been found over the years to produce something special. These may be walled vineyards, or *clos*. The most obvious example is Philipponnat's vertiginous, south-facing Clos des Goisses in the highly rated 99 percent *premier cru* village of Mareuil-sur-Ay. The wines from Clos des Goisses reflect the perfect exposure of this site and are certainly as worthy of attention as other more widely famous single-vineyard champagnes such as Krug's Clos de Mesnil and Clos d'Ambonnay.

New single-vineyard wines are coming onto the market all the time as winemakers learn more about the individual sites they use, partly due to the wider practice of keeping wines with an interesting character for longer before starting the blending process.

» Malolactic fermentation

In between the two stages of fermentation, before bottling, most champagne will go through malolactic fermentation, a biochemical process involving various bacteria that transforms harsh malic acid into softer lactic acid. The majority of producers encourage this process by keeping the wine warm or introducing the lactic bacteria, as it softens the wines and makes them more approachable and less acidic tasting in their youth.

However, certain producers, including Krug, Lanson, Gosset, Bollinger, and Louis Roederer, choose not to put their wines through malolactic fermentation for stylistic reasons. Their wines will therefore tend to taste fresher or, because they take more time to mature, be released after longer aging. The effect of blocking the "malo" is easiest to see in Lanson's nonvintage cuvée Black Label, because it doesn't use any oak in the winemaking process and oaky flavors won't mask the difference.

Blending

Whether it is nonvintage wine, vintage, or a special cuvée, the majority of champagne is a blend (*assemblage*) of several harvests (apart from vintage), of grape varieties, and of the myriad of different *crus* and vineyards across the appellation.

Blends vs single-vineyard

With nearly every other fine wine in Europe, vintage is considered the best. Initially, champagne was no different, but the quality was very inconsistent in this northerly region. The practice of blending was started to combat the inadequacies of a particular year and to promote regularity of style and quality.

Blending is also used to help bring complexity and finesse to the top vintage and prestige styles. The word "cuvée" refers to a specific champagne blend (as well as the juice from the first pressing). The idea is that blending will result in a more complete wine, one that has more different facets, greater complexity, additional nuances of aroma and flavor. In short it will be a better, more interesting wine.

Many Champenois are convinced that great champagne comes only from blending together different component parts, and however interesting single-vineyard or single-varietal wines (those made from just one grape variety) may be, they will never reach the heights achieved by Champagne's greatest blends.

Champagne production

The production process starts with the grape harvest (*vendage*), typically in mid-September. In Champagne the grapes are all picked by hand; mechanical harvesting is not allowed because it is important not to break the skins before pressing. Whole bunches of grapes are collected in small crates to avoid crushing and delivered quickly to the press house.

Pressing

The grapes are then pressed as gently and as quickly as possible, traditionally in a *coquard* basket press, although most producers now use pneumatic presses. The juice from the 8,800 pounds of grapes that make up the *marc* in a standard-size press is separated as it runs off during the pressing process. The cuvée, the best quality, clearer free-run juice produced at the start of the pressing, is kept separate from the darker *taille*, which contains more impurities as a result of the greater pressure gradually exerted in the press. The amount of juice that is drawn off in the cuvée and the *taille* is strictly regulated (2,050 liters and 500 liters respectively).

Before the first alcoholic fermentation takes place, impurities in the pressed grape juice are removed by *débourbage*, a process of settling that allows solid particles to sink to the bottom of the vat, therefore enabling clear juice to be drawn off at the top. This filtration process may be encouraged by chilling the juice in the vat.

Primary fermentation

The clear juice then goes through alcoholic fermentation, in which the natural sugar in the grapes is converted into alcohol while the resultant carbon dioxide is allowed to escape. This produces the base wine. Most often this stage takes place in large stainless-steel vats, although a few famous houses and an increasing band of smaller producers ferment the wines wholly or partially in oak barrels or casks of varying sizes.

At the end of this process the producer will have a collection of still wines (*vins clairs*), perhaps more than two hundred in the case of some of the larger houses. From these they will make their blends for all the different cuvées they produce in any given year, and they may also hold back quantities of these still wines to use as reserve wines for subsequent years (see page 76).

Secondary fermentation

Once a blend is complete, it is put in a bottle: the *liqueur de tirage* (a solution of wine, yeast, and sugar) is added; and the bottles are laid on their side in a cool cellar. The secondary fermentation takes place slowly in the bottle, during which the bubbles are created (the *prise de mousse*) as the carbon dioxide given off is trapped inside. The wine will then be left to age on its lees (the deposits of residual yeast) for a minimum of fifteen months in the case of non-vintage, or three years for vintage champagne.

Riddling

The last stage in the fermentation process is *remuage*, or riddling, the method of removing the yeast deposits left in the bottle. Traditionally, this was done by hand and took about six to eight weeks, but now it mostly takes place in a computer-programmed gyropalette machine. The bottles are placed in the machine and are twisted, shaken, and turned at certain intervals over a few days, eventually finishing in a vertical position, neck down in a wooden container (the *pupitres*), with the yeast deposit settled on the crown cap or cork closure.

Disgorging

The bottles are then ready for the *dégorgement* (disgorging) process, to remove the yeast deposits. The neck of the bottle is frozen, and the cap or cork is removed. Under the pressure that has built up during the fermentation process, a pellet of semi-frozen liquid containing the yeast deposit shoots out. (See pages 49 and 71 for further information.)

Sugar levels

After the *dégorgement* process, the bottle is topped up and the *liqueur de dosage* is added—the amount of sugar added varies depending on the style of champagne being made (see page 14 for the differing dosage levels). The wine is then returned to the cellar to rest and allow the dosage to marry, ideally at least for several months, after which it is ready to go on sale.

The champagne industry

The champagne industry is a complex collection of different producers, generally divided into merchant houses known as *négociant-manipulants* (NM), growers known as *récoltant-manipulants* (RM), and cooperatives, *coopérative-manipulants* (CM). The initials NM, RM, and CM appear in front of a short number on the labels of all champagnes telling you which group has produced any given bottle.

Merchant houses

There are 293 *négociant* houses, the largest of which own the dozen or so major brands that dominate worldwide sales of champagne and include the best-known names, such as Moët & Chandon, Veuve Clicquot, Laurent-Perrier, GH Mumm, Piper Heidsieck, Taittinger, Lanson, and Bollinger.

Although the large *négociant* houses dominate sales of champagne, particularly outside of France, collectively they own only a tenth of Champagne's total vineyard area. The bulk of Champagne's grapes come from the growers who between them farm 90 percent of the appellation's 81,735 acres that are in active production. For example, Champagne's largest group, Louis Vuitton Moët Hennessy (LVMH), has the biggest total vineyard holding among the *négociants*, with some 4,161 acres. This area provides less than one-third of the grapes the company needs to produce its six brands of champagne (Moët & Chandon, Dom Pérignon, Mercier, Ruinart, Veuve Clicquot Ponsardin, and

Krug), more than fifty-five million bottles of which are sold each year. To make up the difference LVMH buys in the production of around another 9,884 acres from across the appellation.

To fuel their brands, most of the big producers have to buy in the majority of the grapes they need from dozens of different growers and co-ops. Houses such as Louis Roederer and Bollinger, which both own enough vineyards to supply about two-thirds of their grape requirements, are rarities.

Growers and co-ops

Of the 15,628 growers currently operating in Champagne, over two-thirds just sell their grapes to the *négociants*. Only around two thousand make and sell wine under their own names.

Many growers have joined forces to form local cooperatives to provide them with central services, such as pressing the grapes, bottling, and even marketing and selling the wine. The cooperatives may also sell grapes and wine on behalf of their grower members to the major *négociant* houses. Out of the 137 cooperatives operating, only 66 actually sell finished wine themselves and 32 of these export their produce, and some make high-quality champagne.

Some smaller cooperative groups have banded together to form "super co-ops," the two largest of which now own significant marques of their own in the shape of Nicolas Feuillatte and Jacquart; the former recently became the fifth-largest-selling champagne on the market.

Bottle sizes

Champagne comes in a variety of bottle sizes, all the way up to the staggeringly large 50-liter Murgatroyd. Most are limited to the sizes below, standard and magnum being the most common. Larger bottles are rare and mostly made for marketing purposes, for special occasions or special cuvées, and are available only from certain producers, such as the 27-liter Primat bottles offered exclusively by Drappier.

Half 37.5 cl ½ bottle

Standard 0.75 liter 1

Magnum 1.5 liters 2

Jeroboam 3 liters 4

Methuselah 6 liters 8

Salmanazar 9 liters 12

Balthazar 12 liters 16

Nebuchadnezzar 15 liters 20

Tasting techniques

When you are tasting champagne with the idea of analyzing it, as opposed to drinking it simply for hedonistic pleasure, you probably want the bottle to be slightly less chilled. Overchilling will dampen down the aromas; cellar temperature of about 50–54°F is preferable to 45–47°F, although the cooler temperature is better for the slow release of the mousse (the stream of fine bubbles that float gently to the surface of the glass). Fill the glass to less than halfway; perhaps around one-third is ideal—enough to be able to assess the mousse and more importantly give plenty of room for the aromas to gather.

Observe the color

You can learn something from the color of the wine, which may vary from the palest lemon or straw in youth to old gold in maturity. Almost colorless suggests a young champagne or perhaps a Blanc de Blancs style. A color moving toward light yellow may indicate more maturity or perhaps a riper vintage. Blends with more Pinot in them also tend to be darker, and a Blanc de Noirs may have a hint of pink in it. A fully mature vintage champagne aged for a decade or more will often take on a rich, golden hue. Rosé champagnes may range in intensity from the merest hint of color (sometimes called "partridge eye") to opal or copper or even a light ruby red that might be mistaken for a glass of Beaujolais.

Bubbles

It is often said that a steady, persistent stream of fine, small bubbles (the mousse) is a sign of quality in champagne. However, the speed, persistence, and size of the bubbles is more likely to be affected by the type of glass you use and its cleanliness than a clear sign of inherent quality. You can, however, assess the mousse reasonably accurately on tasting: the smaller the bubbles, the smoother the mousse feels in the mouth. The tiniest bubbles help create a creamy, silky texture on the finish.

Aromas

As for champagne's aromas, we can perhaps helpfully put them into several groups.

Floral aromas: lime blossom, violet, orange blossom, hawthorn.

Fruity aromas: citrus ones, such as lemon, grapefruit, lime, orange; yellow fruit, such as peach, apricot, nectarine, quince; exotic fruit, including mango, banana, coconut, lychees; and red or black fruit, such as raspberry, strawberry, blackcurrant, plum.

Vegetal aromas: fresh almonds, cut grass, truffle.

Dried fruit aromas: hazelnuts, raisins, dried figs.

Epicurean aromas: brioche, vanilla, butter, toast, biscuit notes, honey, gingerbread, candied fruit, mocha, white chocolate, mushroom, smoke, spices (such as cinnamon), notes of decay and torrefaction.

While it is possible to generalize about the typical flavors that each of the three main grape varieties tend to bring to a champagne blend, it is also worth pointing out that you are likely to come across exceptions to the rule.

Words from the wise

W. Craig Cooper Beverage
director, Pops for Champagne,
Chicago, IL

» Handle with care

More often than not, when I come across a bottle of
champagne that has less than desirable flavors or
aromas, the defect can be attributed to improper
handling or storage somewhere along its path to my
table. Champagne is a delicate wine and thus can be
more susceptible than others to the damaging effects
of heat, vibration, and light. Patronize bars whose
owners know how to handle and rotate their stocks
properly, and do your best to learn the bottle's
provenance (the fewer hands that have touched it,
from the producer's cellar to your own, the better).

As with any wine, a cool, quiet, dark place is
best for storage, but don't make the mistake of
keeping a bottle chilled in your refrigerator for "that
special occasion." Prolonged refrigeration dries out
the cork, causing shrinkage and spoiling the wine.
Disgorgement dates are becoming more common
these days. Pay attention to them but don't see them
as some sort of expiration date. For me, they are
much more likely to offer up the notion of waiting a
few months before popping a cork.

Palate

Our sense of smell is infinitely more developed than our sense of taste. Humans can identify four taste flavors: saltiness, sweetness, acidity, and bitterness. Some would add umami, which has long fascinated experimental chefs such as Heston Blumenthal and also strikes a note with some of Champagne's top winemakers, including Dom Pérignon's chef de cave, Richard Geoffroy.

When you are tasting champagne, you are first looking at the initial "attack"—the crispness, freshness and zip, the balance of fruit and acidity— and the mouthfeel you experience, partly affected by the mousse and the fizziness of the wine. Look then for the wine's structure and intensity: is it light, delicate, ethereal or perhaps rich, full-bodied, and structured? Is it nicely balanced, rounded, and harmonious? Is the palate texture creamy and silky smooth or edgy, sharp, even aggressive? What about the maturity? Does it have those yeasty, bready autolytic characters of fine aged champagne? Is there any hint of oak or of slow oxidation? Finally, does it show many of these facets together, plus a complex array of attractive flavors and aromas with a finish that stays in your mouth for a long time? If it does, this suggests real class.

» International marques

Dominant exporters

There are currently 297 *négociant* houses operating in Champagne, 232 of which exported wine to markets outside France in 2009; between them they accounted for nearly 87 percent of all export sales. The largest three brands—Moët & Chandon, Veuve Clicquot, and GH Mumm—shipped a third of the *négociants* total exports.

The largest houses tend to have their cellars based either in Reims or Épernay, although their physical location doesn't tell us much about the style of wine they produce, as these larger *négociants* buy in grapes from growers spread all over the region.

Reims

Ruinart

4, Rue des Crayères, 51100 Reims

Tel: +33 (0)3 26 77 51 51 www.ruinart.com

Ruinart was founded by Nicolas Ruinart in 1729 and is the oldest producer of champagne still operating today. Ruinart is part of the LVMH group, but its wines are still relatively unknown outside France. It is particularly renowned for its Blanc de Blancs, all-Chardonnay styles, which reach a fabulous peak in the vintage prestige cuvée Dom Ruinart. Its pink counterpart—Dom Ruinart Rosé—is the most expensive and exclusive line in the present range.

The Dom Ruinart wines tend to improve with a little further aging after release. They are essentially food wines that work very well with white meats, veal, and feathered game.

» ### Dom Ruinart Blanc de Blancs 2002

Unusually, and unlike most great all-Chardonnay champagnes, the grapes used for this champagne don't come solely from *grands crus* villages in the Côte des Blancs. A third comes from the Montagne de Reims villages of Sillery, Puisleux, Verzenay, and Mailly. Pale gold in color with developed aromas of brioche and toast, this wine seems rich, ripe, and forward.

» ### Dom Ruinart Rosé 1996

A rich coppery pink, Dom Ruinart Rosé tends to be launched a year or so later than its white counterpart, but despite that this wine is still extraordinarily youthful. Again, it is Chardonnay-driven with no black grapes in the blend, just the addition of between 15 and 20 percent red wine, all *grand cru* Pinot Noir Bouzy Rouge.

Lanson

66, Rue de Courlancy, 51100 Reims

Tel: +33 (0)3 26 78 50 50 www.lanson.com

This famous house has recently celebrated its 250th anniversary. Since being purchased by the Boizel Chanoine group in 2006, the wines have improved and it looks poised to return to its former glory. Lanson's strength is its vintage Gold Label wines, which after a more difficult period *sans vineyards* in the early nineties (when the brand name was sold on without the vineyards), has returned to impressive form with the 1998 and especially the 1999 releases.

» **Lanson (Gold Label) Vintage 2002**

The vintage release Gold Label Brut Vintage 2002 is in impressively good form after more than a decade of aging gracefully. It has a nicely developed biscuity note and silky intensity.

» **Lanson Noble Cuvée Brut Vintage 1999**

This is the original Noble Cuvée prestige style (there are now three), usually a classy, nicely balanced, understated ratio of 70:30 Chardonnay/Pinot Noir blend. Because it is not that well known it is great value, too. It has a very fresh, lively sherbetty fizz with an attractive waxy, creamy, palate texture building. This wine still has a long future ahead of it.

Veuve Clicquot Ponsardin

1, Place des Droits de l'Homme, 51100 Reims

Tel: +33 (0)3 26 89 53 90 www.veuve-clicquot.com

Veuve Clicquot is perhaps the most successful house in terms of creating the right image. It is certainly the brand most admired by other large producers. The downside of the iconic status that the Yellow Label nonvintage cuvée has acquired is that the volume has shot up and it is hard to keep quality consistently high when producing fifteen million bottles a year. The full-bodied Pinot Noir–dominated house style can best be seen in the fine vintage releases over the past few decades, which also age extremely well.

Words from the wise

Didier Mariotti Chef de Cave,
GH Mumm, Reims, France

» The correct temperature

Champagne is a wine, even though it's also a sparkling wine. I think people always serve champagne too cold and, just as with white table wine, this will emphasize the freshness. As with other wines, we have to select the right temperature and the best glass according to the blend—we don't use the same glass for red Burgundy and red Bordeaux.

When it comes to our prestige cuvée R Lalou, for example, which is a blend of roughly equal parts of Chardonnay and Pinot Noir, it depends which side of the blend you want to emphasize. The side I prefer depends on the time of day, on my mood, and the drinking occasion—whether I drink it as an aperitif or paired with food. The temperature I drink it at and the glass I use depends on these factors. A cooler temperature (46–50°F) will emphasize the Chardonnay in the blend, while a warmer temperature (57°F) will show the Pinot Noir side.

Veuve Clicquot Brut Vintage Réserve 2002

Originally launched in September 2007, this wine is still available and has developed very attractively. A blend dominated by black grapes (60 percent Pinot Noir, 7 percent Pinot Meunier), it has a rounded and rich, full-bodied style that is now showing a creamy palate with distinctive biscuity notes and good mouthfeel. It will develop further complexity for perhaps another two to three years.

Veuve Clicquot Cave Privée Rosé 1989

EXPERT Essential From a ripe year, with lower acidity, this pale copper-pink 1989 rosé was a vintage that many houses predicted wouldn't last that long, but this rosé remains remarkably fresh. There are roasted coffee and mocha notes, strawberry fruit on the initial palate, then a meaty, savory mid-palate, and a long finish.

Veuve Clicquot La Grande Dame 2004

Luxury cuvée La Grande Dame is less vinous and more elegant than the meaty Vintage Réserve style, thanks to larger amounts of Chardonnay in the blend (around 40 percent) and the fact that it is made solely of Blanc de Blancs *grand cru*.

Louis Roederer

21, Boulevard Lundy, 51053 Reims

Tel: +33 (0)3 26 40 42 11
www.champagne-roederer.com

One of the most celebrated houses in Champagne, and still entirely owned by the Rouzaud family, Roederer's wines are particularly renowned for their elegance and finesse. The quality of the range is partly due to the highly rated 539-acre vineyard estate, much of it located in the best *grands crus*, which supplies about two-thirds of the house's grape needs.

» Louis Roederer Brut Premier NV

This is a particularly fine nonvintage cuvée. It has an elegant, complex style with finesse and structure that is underpinned by the use of reserve wines from three different harvests, which are matured in oak casks for three to five years. It is aged for forty months before release but, like other top-quality nonvintage champagne, you could cellar it for a couple of years more.

» Louis Roederer Cristal 2005

EXPERT *Essential* Originally created exclusively for Tsar Alexander II of Russia in 1876, prestige cuvée Cristal, in its clear bottle and gold cellophane wrap, is one of the wines that defines this luxury sector of the market (along with Krug and Dom Pérignon) and is perhaps the most sought after in the appellation. The wine is subtle yet complex and all about balance: balancing fine acidity, flavors, and mouthfeel. Its power and intensity are disguised by a seductive, silky, textural cloak. Initially attractive

on release, with good cellaring the wine will develop layers of complexity over several years.

» **Louis Roederer Blanc de Blancs Vintage 2004**
Half the price of Cristal but not half the quality, this champagne is very pale, intense, startlingly fresh, and linear in its youth. With time it develops into one of the most delightful wines in the range.

GH Mumm

29, Rue du Champ de Mars, 51100 Reims

Tel: +33 (0)3 26 49 59 69 www.mumm.com

After a difficult period and several changes of ownership, GH Mumm's range continues to show steady improvement under the management of Pernod Ricard, a trend set in motion by winemaker Dominique Demarville (now at Veuve Clicquot) and carried on by his successor, Didier Mariotti.

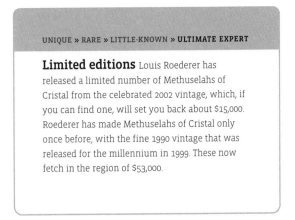

UNIQUE » RARE » LITTLE-KNOWN » **ULTIMATE EXPERT**

Limited editions Louis Roederer has released a limited number of Methuselahs of Cristal from the celebrated 2002 vintage, which, if you can find one, will set you back about $15,000. Roederer has made Methuselahs of Cristal only once before, with the fine 1990 vintage that was released for the millennium in 1999. These now fetch in the region of $53,000.

» Mumm de Cramant

This very pale, delicate, fresh all-Chardonnay cuvée is made at a lower pressure in the *crémant* style (see page 95; it used to be named Crémant de Cramant), which gives it a softer texture in the mouth. It is actually made from one vintage, but, because it is designed to be consumed while crisp and young, it doesn't have a year on the label—by law vintage styles have to be aged for a minimum of three years before release.

» R Lalou 1998

Mumm's prestige cuvée, René Lalou, was discontinued at the end of the eighties, but its natural successor R Lalou, made from the 1998 vintage, was first released in 2007 and is based on the same company-owned vineyard parcels. An elegant wine with an initial emphasis on citrus fruits and the freshness from the north-facing slopes of Verzy and Verzenay still noticeable, it has more aging capacity yet. The excellent 1999 vintage was also released in early 2011.

Charles Heidsieck

12, Allée du Vignoble, 51100 Reims

Tel: +33 (0)3 26 84 43 50
www.charlesheidsieck.com

There are three brands in Champagne with the name Heidsieck, but Charles Heidsieck, the youngest, is the one to look for if you are hunting for top-quality wines right across the range. Established by Charles-Camille Heidsieck, the firm was bought by what is now the Rémy-Cointreau group in 1985.

The group kept on winemaker Daniel Thibault, widely viewed as the best of his generation, with a remit to make Charles Heidsieck Brut Réserve a top-class cuvée. This and other Charles Heidsieck wines have gone on to win numerous awards, and happily his successor, Régis Camus, is continuing in the same award-winning ways.

» Charles Heidsieck Brut Réserve NV

EXPERT Essential The secret behind Thibault's success in creating this cuvée was in using large quantities of quality reserve wines in each blend (up to 40 percent), which is double what most houses typically use, and then in aging these very fine blends for longer before release. The current release has 40 percent reserve wine of between two and ten years old in the blend. There are notes of fresh-baked bread and ripe peachy fruit, a sherbetty lift, and an intensely creamy soft mid-palate and long finish.

» Charles Heidsieck Blanc des Millénaires 1995

Exclusively composed of Chardonnay from the Côte des Blancs, this magical wine from the great 1995 vintage is at a glorious peak of maturity. Ripe and opulent on the nose, with notes of marzipan, hazelnuts, and white chocolate, the palate is rich, creamy, and silky.

» Charles Heidsieck Brut Vintage 2000

This vintage champagne really is made only in the best years—1996, 1995, and 1990 precede it. At first release, in late 2007, although it showed lovely balance and rich texture, it gave only a hint of the glories to come in maturity. Now a burnished gold color, it has opened up; the palate texture has softened, with notes of vanilla and mocha starting to develop.

》 ### Charles Heidsieck Brut Rosé NV

The first cuvée of this wine was released at the end of 2008. A deliciously fruity, beautifully balanced, creamy-textured champagne, it is a worthy partner to Charles Heidsieck Brut Réserve, which has been one of the best and most consistent nonvintage cuvées on the market for the past nineteen years.

Taittinger

9, Place Saint-Nicaise, 51100 Reims

Tel: +33 (0)3 26 85 45 35 www.taittinger.com

041

Pierre-Emmanuel Taittinger is the latest family member to run this famous house founded in 1931, whose 563 acres of vineyard (including holdings in six *grands crus* in the Côte des Blancs) provide a significant proportion of its needs. Chardonnay plays an important part in the range and reaches a high point in the prestige cuvée Comtes de Champagne Blanc de Blancs.

》 ### Comtes de Champagne Blanc de Blancs 2002

EXPERT *Essential* This wine is an all-Chardonnay cuvée that really needs more than a decade to show its true colors and lush palate.

It works particularly well in riper vintages. This example is classy and already showing an attractive biscuity note and silken texture, but it will get better still.

›› Prélude Grands Crus NV

This is an award-winning 50/50 blend of Chardonnay from the top-rated vineyards of Avize and Le Mesnil-sur-Oger and Pinot Noir from Bouzy and Ambonnay, which with extra aging shows a rich, mellow fullness and a satisfyingly long finish.

Épernay

Moët & Chandon

20, Avenue de Champagne, 51200 Épernay

Tel: +33 (0)3 26 51 20 20 www.moet.com

Given that Moët Brut Impérial is the top-selling champagne worldwide and is produced in very large quantities (close to thirty million bottles a year), the quality is impressively consistent and always seems to go up a notch in magnum. Moët's vintage wines (called Grand Vintage) are quite a step up and in top years, such as 1996, 2002, and 2004, represent one of the best bargains in champagne.

›› Moët & Chandon Grand Vintage Brut 2002

Moët released this vintage out of sequence after the 2003 version and now plans to age all vintage releases seven years in the cellar rather than five, according to chef de cave Benoît Gouez. The blend of Grand Vintage 2002 is 51 percent Chardonnay, 26 percent Pinot Noir, and 23 percent Pinot Meunier. Initially it shows ripe stone fruit aromas with notes of fresh brioche. Fine balancing acidity suggests it has a long future and will develop attractively, gathering more complexity.

Dom Pérignon

www.domperignon.com

Owned by Moët, but with a separate winemaking team led by chef de cave Richard Geoffroy since 1990, this is *the* original prestige cuvée champagne. Usually first released seven years after the harvest from which it was made, if you consume it immediately, as sadly the majority of consumers do, you will be missing much of the point of the wine, as its flavors and complexity develop only gradually over time. Try to give it at least three or four years extra cellaring. In recognition of the wine's slow development, Moët re-releases the wine twice under the Oenothèque Collection at around twelve and twenty-plus years in what Geoffroy calls its second and third "plenitude."

» **Dom Pérignon 2000**
Geoffroy describes this wine as a "paradoxical vintage: fresh yet mature, austere but seductive," and it does seem quite opulent and forward as an aperitif, but the minute you eat food with it, the underlying acidity that will give it a very long life comes to the fore.

In the details

The flavors and aromas that
develop during extra aging

» Stages of aging

Good champagne, particularly vintage champagne, ages very well and typically goes through several phases of development, from zingy, fresh, and fruity to tertiary notes such as chocolate, mushroom, and leather. At Dom Pérignon, for example, chef de cave Richard Geoffroy releases his wines at three optimal moments: the first after seven years of aging, the second at twelve to fifteen years, the third after two decades.

The aromas change dramatically, initially tending toward notes of fresh brioche, citrus fruits, sweet spices, and occasionally honey. The second stage extends to classic characteristics of maturity: aromas of toast, hazelnuts, biscuits, malt, chocolate, and spices. Beyond twenty years, the aromatic range takes on a new dimension and becomes more exotic and intriguing, veering from the classic path to evoke unusual sensations, almost like perfume: sandalwood, musk, new leather, a blend of oriental spices, blond tobacco, and white truffles.

» Dom Pérignon Oenothèque 1995

Oenothèque 1995 and 1975 are a particularly impressive pair. The former, disgorged in February 2007, will continue to open up but is already very rich and lush with some ripe mango fruit and a creamy vanilla palate, although there's still plenty of freshness to give it balance.

» Dom Pérignon Oenothèque 1975

The 1975 has an altogether more perfumed, honeyed, floral nose and a meaty, savory intensity. It is not big and powerful, but subtle and complex and

UNIQUE » RARE » LITTLE-KNOWN » **ULTIMATE EXPERT**

Bespoke cuvée In the summer of 2008, Perrier-Jouët Belle released Epoque Blanc de Blancs 2000 "By and For," which cost $53,000 for a case of twelve bottles. Just one hundred cases of this "bespoke" cuvée were offered worldwide and only to customers in the USA, Britain, Japan, China, Russia, Switzerland, and France. As part of the package buyers met with chef de cave Hervé Deschamps at Perrier-Jouët's Maison Belle Epoque in Épernay to customize their wine to their own personal taste. This involved, after tasting the various options available, picking the exact dosage to be used in the *liqueur d'expedition,* added after the wine is disgorged and before it is given its final cork.

demonstrates dramatically what those who drink the 2000 quickly may be missing.

Perrier-Jouët

28, Avenue de Champagne, 51200 Épernay

Tel: +33 (0)3 26 53 38 00 www.perrier-jouet.com

Perrier-Jouët is best known for the Art Nouveau flower motif (designed by Emile Gallé) that adorns its prestige cuvée Belle Epoque, arguably the most distinctive champagne bottle around. Now reaping the benefit of Pernod Ricard's investment, Perrier-Jouët's range is proving more consistent with the straight vintage and Blason Rosé being the best buys, while Belle Epoque has been on good form since the mid-1990s.

>> ### Perrier-Jouët Belle Epoque Brut 2002

At the launch of this cuvée from the top-class 2002 vintage, everyone was surprised about how lush, forward, and hedonistically seductive the wine immediately seemed, and some have doubted its staying power, although ripe vintages like 1976 and 1989 often have remarkable longevity. Older vintages of Belle Epoque (1998, 1996, and 1995) in magnum and Jeroboam bottles offer delightful complexity.

>> **Perrier-Jouët Blason Rosé NV**

This exuberantly fruity and stylish rosé is not at all well known yet often seems more attractive than the pink Belle Epoque. It is full of primary red-berry fruit, with quite a soft creamy palate but enough acidity to keep it fresh.

Pol Roger

1, Rue Henri Lelarge, 51206 Épernay

Tel: +33 (0)3 26 59 58 00   www.polroger.com

Pol Roger was Winston Churchill's favorite brand of champagne. Over the last decade, the company has re-invested in improved production facilities, employed Krug's former winemaker Dominique Petit, and gained access to more high-quality *grand cru* fruit. As a result, all of its wines have been performing consistently well (not just the excellent vintage styles that have always been its strength).

>> **Pol Roger Brut Réserve**

A soft and powerful three-way blend of Chardonnay and Pinots Noir and Meunier. Extra lees aging (see page 44) before release—the cuvée is typically blended with a good proportion of reserve wine from the previous two vintages—help rich, ripe, yeasty aromas develop.

>> **Pol Roger Brut Vintage 2000**

Rich and full-bodied in style, this 60/40 blend of Pinot Noir and Chardonnay has fragrant, perfumed fruit, while the palate is rich, yet fine-grained with a lovely concentration. There's a hint of spice with an attractive biscuity note before a long finish.

» Pol Roger Blanc de Chardonnay 1999

This is a superb all-Chardonnay vintage champagne capable of long aging and able to stand up to quite robust food. In a magnum, it is still incredibly fresh, with a lifted grapefruit acidity but also a creamy texture developing—this one is ready to drink but can be stored for another one or two years.

» Pol Roger Cuvée Sir Winston Churchill 1998

EXPERT Essential The family is curiously reticent about the exact make-up of this celebrated cuvée. Initially it has attractive notes of brioche, toasted almonds, and ripe stone fruit with a luscious fleshy texture tempered by fine acidity. It is a big, full-bodied, gloriously rich wine.

049

Recently Disgorged (RD)

RD is a concept that was first developed by Madame Lily Bollinger to show off the exceptional aging capabilities of Bollinger's wines with the 1952 vintage (released in 1961). RD is Bollinger's Grande Année blend kept longer on it lees to heighten its aromatics. At disgorgement the wine gets a lighter dosage of between 3 and 4 g/l and is then released after three months so those who want a fresher style can drink it soon after disgorgement. RD is a Bollinger trademark, so other houses use terms like "late disgorgement" or *dégorgement tardif*.

Other regions

Bollinger

16, Rue Jules Lobet 51160 Aÿ

Tel: +33 (0)3 26 53 33 66
www.champagne-bollinger.com

This deeply traditional, family-run house, based in the *grand cru* village of Aÿ, controls a 403-acre vineyard estate that supplies two-thirds of its grape needs. Bollinger's commitment to the highest production standards was set out in its Charter of Ethics and Quality, published in 1992, the stringent rules of which have become a blueprint for quality in the region. All the Bollinger wines gather richness and complexity as they age, particularly the vintage.

» ### Bollinger Special Cuvée

The weighty, complex style of this champagne is rich with a long finish but has shown increasing elegance as well as power. One of the top five NV cuvées in terms of consistency and quality, the wine is a blend of two recent harvests with 10 percent of an older reserve wine, some of which may date back fifteen to twenty years.

» ### Bollinger La Grande Année Rosé 1999

It is hard to find a more beautifully balanced vintage rosé, with its raspberry fruit, creamy texture, charm, and elegance. The 2002 is also a class act, but it could perhaps benefit from aging a year or two more, while the 1999 will provide great drinking pleasure for several years now.

Words from the wise

Roger Jones Owner, The Harrow, Wiltshire, UK

» Further aging

I am keen to lay down certain multivintage champagnes for further aging, not just single-vintage—but it has to be the right wine to warrant this treatment, for example Krug Grande Cuvée, Gosset Grande Réserve, and Jacquesson Cuvée 733, because these all offer fantastic value and do improve considerably with more time in the bottle. Our experienced champagne-drinking clientele do appreciate the difference they see in the glass.

Don't be hesitant of buying older vintage wines like 1996, which can age terrifically. With vintage champagne you don't have to pay much more to get a wine that has already been aged considerably longer before you buy it. Veuve Clicquot Vintage Réserve costs only about 30 percent more than their nonvintage. On first release Dom Pérignon tends to need a few years before it starts to develop, but it is definitely well worth the wait.

» Bollinger La Grande Année 2000 (and 2002)

 One of the best examples of what has turned out to be a very attractive, generally soft, ripe, and forward-drinking vintage, this wine is hardly on its last legs and in magnum has a long future ahead of it. Typical yeasty, autolytic notes, with more than a hint of Marmite, preface a soft, buttery, weighty palate, though there is nothing clumsy here—just vinous pleasure. The beautifully refined, balanced, more classical 2002 Grand Année, potentially a very long keeper, will follow.

Laurent-Perrier

Domaine Laurent-Perrier, 51150 Tours-sur-Marne

Tel: +33 (0)3 26 58 91 22 www.laurentperrier.com

Laurent-Perrier is probably still best known for its trend-setting nonvintage rosé, packaged in a distinctive bottle that kickstarted the popularity of pink champagne. The company also boasts the most widely available *nondosé* (bone-dry) style of champagne in ultra brut. Given the large number of such wines now being made, Laurent-Perrier may claim to have started another significant trend.

052

>> **Laurent-Perrier Brut NV**

This has a soft, light, delicate style with no harsh edges. It is easy to drink and expertly made, designed to leave you wanting more, not aiming to be too characterful.

>> **Grand Siècle La Cuvée NV**

This prestige cuvée is unusual in being a blend of three different harvests—the version I sampled was based on 1999, 1997, and 1996 harvests, as well as a roughly 50/50 blend of Chardonnay and Pinot Noir. Subtle and delicate, and not at all muscular, it tends to go buttery rather than toasty and yeasty with more age.

>> **Grand Siècle Cuvée Alexandra Rosé Vintage 1998**

A gorgeous coppery pink, this rosé has heady floral scents and hints of raspberry fruit that develop into richer black fruit with a little time in the glass. This is a classic, elegant rosé, delicate but persistent with great finesse—a luxurious indulgence.

Duval-Leroy

69, Avenue de Bammental, 51130 Vertus

Tel: +33 (0)3 26 52 10 75 www.duval-leroy.com

Carol Duval runs this excellent but underrated family-owned house based in the village of Vertus in the Côte des Blancs. The quality of its vintage cuvées is built around the 494 acres of prime vineyards it owns, which are mostly planted with Chardonnay. It has shown considerable innovation over the past decade, releasing a string of interesting wines under its Authentis range.

>> **Blanc de Chardonnay Brut Vintage 1999**
A rich, golden yellow gives a hint of ripe, succulent fruit in this attractively mature vintage that offers very enjoyable drinking now.

>> **Clos des Bouveries 2004**
Part of the Authentis range, this is a single-vineyard, all-Chardonnay cuvée that comes from a low-yielding 8.6-acre plot at the southern end of the village of Vertus. The third release of this wine is big, ripe, and concentrated, although perhaps lacking some of the vivacity of the original 2002.

>> **Femme de Champagne 1996**
EXPERT Essential This is the prestige cuvée of the house, made from the superripe 1996 vintage, which also boasted the highest acidity levels in recent times. This piercingly fresh and citrusy wine took quite a few years to come around, but ripe fruit and racy acidity are finally in balance and the result is an exciting, tongue-tingling fizz with an underlying richness emerging.

Billecart-Salmon

40, Rue Carnot, 51160 Mareuil-sur-Ay

Tel: +33 (0)3 26 52 60 22
www.champagne-billecart.fr

François Roland-Billecart is the seventh generation of the family to run this highly regarded house. Over the past few years, the company has increased its annual production to around

1.7 million bottles, thanks to access to an extra 198 acres of vineyard owned by Jean-Jacques Frey, who has a 45 percent share in the house. While Billecart is particularly admired for its rosé wines, its white vintage wines are arguably the stars, capable of very long aging and developing deliciously well.

» Brut Rosé NV

A gorgeous pale pink, this rosé is positioned very much in the refined, understated, delicately fruity aperitif camp and has many admirers. Initially very fresh, it develops an attractive creaminess if aged for a year or so.

UNIQUE » RARE » LITTLE-KNOWN » **ULTIMATE EXPERT**

Ungrafted vines At the end of the nineteenth century, the phylloxera pest (an aphid that attacks the vine roots) destroyed most of the Champagne vineyards. Most vines were replanted on American rootstock to protect them from this disease, but certain areas were unaffected, including three tiny plots (1.4 acres in all) of Pinot Noir—two in the *grand cru* village of Ay and the other in Bouzy. The Bollinger Vieilles Vignes Françaises 2000 is produced from these three plots of ungrafted Pinot Noir. Because of the very low yields, just 3,766 bottles of this Blanc de Noirs style were produced, which cost in the region of $470 to $580 a bottle.

» Brut Blanc de Blancs 1999

EXPERT *Essential* It says much about the keeping qualities of the Billecart wines that this cuvée was only starting to reveal its real pedigree and finesse two or three years after its first release. This is partly down to the blend of just three top *grands crus* sites: Cramant for finesse, Avize for its power, and Mesnil-sur-Oger for its structure and longevity. As a result it will still develop happily for another decade and may even match the quality and complexity of a recently consumed bottle of the fine vintage 1990. Quince-like aromas highlight the ripeness of the harvest, and the palate has a burnished richness likely to turn more chocolatey with time.

» Le Clos Saint-Hilaire 1998

Billecart launched this single-vineyard wine (100 percent Pinot Noir that comes from a 2.5-acre walled vineyard close to the winery in Mareuil-sur-Ay) with the 1995 vintage released in 2003. This cuvée impresses on every level, although the previous 1996 cuvée was a hard act to follow in terms of sheer intensity. A golden yellow hue, it shows ripe peachy fruit notes, impressive richness, and concentration while retaining a fine, lively, refreshing acidity.

» Regional marques

Regional influence

Although four of the smaller *négociant* houses are located in or on the outskirts of the city of Reims, and Alfred Gratien is in Épernay, most of the others are based in villages or *crus* that play a central part in the production of their wine and tell us something about them. These houses would consider themselves small-scale artisan producers. The vast majority makes fewer than one million bottles a year, some considerably less.

Montagne de Reims

Cattier

6/11, Rue Dom Pérignon,
51500 Chigny-les-Roses

Tel: +33 (0)3 26 03 42 11 www.cattier.com

This family-run house based in Chigny-les-Roses, just to the south of Reims, owns forty-nine acres of vineyards, much of it rated *premier cru*. Today, Cattier has become better known for its Armand de Brignac brand, with its stand-out glitzy packaging in gold, silver, and shocking pink, respectively, for the brut, Blanc de Blancs, and rosé styles it comes in.

» **Armand de Brignac NV Brut**
This was first launched in 2006 and, like Clos du Moulin, it is a blend of three harvests, mainly 2005, with smaller equal amounts of 2003 and 2002. It has

a very low dosage of just 6 g/l so is extra brut in style. While it is fresh and lifted, thanks to a generous splash of *grand cru* Chardonnay, it is rounded out partly due to the *liqueur de dosage* being aged in oak casks. It has decent length, too.

Henriot

81, Rue Coquebert, 51100 Reims

Tel: +33 (0)3 26 89 53 00
www.champagne-henriot.com

The Henriot family has been in Champagne since the sixteenth century. The present head of the company, Joseph Henriot, established Veuve Clicquot's modern reputation before returning to the family business in the nineties. He subsequently spread his family interests further south to Burgundy, where he bought and restored the fortunes of Bouchard Père et Fils and William Fèvre. Henriot's champagnes, however, are relatively unknown, but they are all well made and the vintage wines and deluxe line Cuvée des Enchanteleurs are potential gems that age beautifully.

» Vintage Brut 1996

This is a rerelease of a fine vintage that had a magical combination of very ripe fruit and unusually high acidity. It has now developed gloriously, showing lovely concentration and creamy depth, though it is still enlivened by racy acidity, so there is no great hurry to drink it up.

» Cuvée des Enchanteleurs 1998

EXPERT *Essential* This is a champagne to linger over, a wine at, or near, the height of its opulent power.

It should be sipped and savored on a sunny afternoon in the garden. A blend of 55 percent Chardonnay and 45 percent Pinot Noir with a mature toasty nose of heady complexity, it has notes of zesty, spicy, exotic fruit that give way to a sumptuous Meursault-like richness on the palate and a long chocolatey finish.

Krug

5, Rue de Coquebert, 51100 Reims

Tel: +33 (0)3 26 84 44 20 www.krug.com

Olivier Krug is the sixth generation of the Krug family to head up this famous house. Producer of the most exclusive and highest-priced wines in the appellation, Krug champagnes are renowned for their longevity and rich, vinous style. Unlike any other house in Champagne, it only produces wines that fit within the prestige cuvée sector, and all retail for over $150 a bottle—some considerably more.

» Krug Grande Cuvée

The Krug Grande Cuvée is a multivintage blend, with even the youngest component aged at least five years on its yeast lees; some of its reserve elements are twenty years old. The style is distinctively rich and developed, with secondary aromas of brioche, vanilla, mocha, as well as smoky, spicy notes coming partly from fermentation in small oak casks and long aging. Complexity is added by the significant amount (sometimes as high as 50 percent) of reserve wine in the blend.

Vintage 1996

One of the greatest Krug vintage wines ever made, this is an impressive, supercharged, and superconcentrated champagne, which shows off all the best facets of this potentially great vintage—amazing vitality borne of very high acidity and great richness from one of the ripest harvests on record. The finish is powerful, penetratingly vivid, and very long indeed in the mouth.

Krug Clos du Mesnil 1996

EXPERT *Essential* This is a single-vineyard wine from a 4.6-acre Chardonnay vineyard in Le Mesnil-sur-Oger. With the Krug Vintage 1996 being so impressive in every way, it is very hard to imagine that the Clos du Mesnil 1996 could surpass it, but tasted side by side that is precisely what it does. The palate intensity is startling, the texture silken.

Notes of ripe exotic fruit and lime are cut with mouthwatering acidity before a creamy richness fills the mouth and leads to a long, powerful finish. It has even more to reveal over the next decade or so.

Clos d'Ambonnay 1996

As we have seen, 1996 was a very particular year in Champagne, generally producing wines with intense acidity and high ripeness levels. Both show up in the Clos d'Ambonnay, which at first appears rich, ripe, and evolved with developed toasty, bready aromas. On the palate, however, it is still intensely fresh and citrusy and has a very long life ahead—a couple of decades or more. The price has actually dropped a little since the original lauch to between $1,800 and $2,100 a bottle.

Champagne Marguet Père & Fils

1, Place Barancourt, 51150 Ambonnay

Tel: +33 (0)3 26 53 78 61
www.champagne-marguet.fr

Benoit Marguet is a fifth-generation vine grower, who has set out in a new direction: converting to organic farming wherever possible, plowing by horse, using 90 percent oak fermentation, and seeking to make wines with a strong individual character.

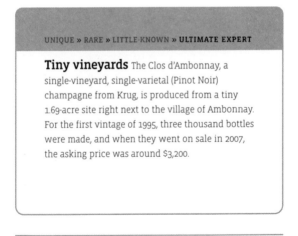

UNIQUE » RARE » LITTLE-KNOWN » **ULTIMATE EXPERT**

Tiny vineyards The Clos d'Ambonnay, a single-vineyard, single-varietal (Pinot Noir) champagne from Krug, is produced from a tiny 1.69-acre site right next to the village of Ambonnay. For the first vintage of 1995, three thousand bottles were made, and when they went on sale in 2007, the asking price was around $3,200.

>> **Blanc de Noirs Brut NV**

This is a blend of 75 percent Pinot Noir and 25 percent Pinot Meunier Blanc de Noirs. It is attractively fruited with big flavors, mineral notes, a biscuity texture, and good mouthfeel—an expressive and impressive wine with lots of life and energy.

>> **Grand Cru Rosé Brut NV**

There is just Ambonnay and Bouzy fruit (70 percent Chardonnay and 30 percent Pinot Noir) in this pretty, pale-pink champagne with orange highlights; the color comes from a 12 percent portion vinified as red wine, plus 1 percent from *saignée*. Made in a clean, fresh, lifted style—thanks partly to a portion of Cramant and Le Mesnil-sur-Oger Chardonnay—the wine also boasts a dense black-fruit component.

>> **Grand Cru Brut Millésime 2002**

This is a blend of 70 percent Chardonnay and 30 percent Pinot Noir made entirely from *grands crus* in the Montagne de Reims and Côte des Blancs. With rich, plump, peachy fruit and a velvety soft texture, this also has some spiciness and mineral intensity.

Bruno Paillard

Avenue de Champagne, 51100 Reims

Tel: +33 (0)3 26 36 20 22
www.champagnebrunopaillard.com

This is a thoroughly modern house: its "cellars" are all aboveground in a large, temperature-controlled warehouse, using the latest technology. Bruno Paillard, who established his new house at the age of twenty-seven in 1981, quickly gained a reputation for the quality of his own wines. Since 1985, Paillard's wines have shown the date of disgorgement, an enlightened policy that more and more quality producers are following today.

» **Brut Première Cuvée NV**

This is an elegant, fresh, citrus-tinged style (although only one-third Chardonnay) that boasts an underlying depth and richness, thanks to good use of reserve wines, which make up between 20 and 50 percent of the blend. This wine can age impressively, going buttery rich with spicy gingerbread notes, as a tasting of this wine (based on the 1995 harvest with a dozen years post-disgorgement age) showed recently.

» **Rosé Première Cuvée NV**

A lovely, delicate, pale onion-skin color, this lightly fruity rosé has real class and finesse—something to savor on a warm summer's evening *alfresco* or as a special aperitif. It is served in some of the best hotel bars in Paris, including Le Meurice.

» **Grande Cuvée Nec Plus Ultra 1996**

This prestige line is given the extra aging a *grand cru* luxury cuvée deserves before release but rarely gets in today's climate. It is sourced from seven *grands crus* and is barrel-fermented, with two years post-disgorgement rest before release and a low dosage of just 4 g/l. Waxy mouth texture, toastiness, and a hint of honey come out as it opens in the glass.

» **Brut Millésime 1996 Blanc de Blancs**

EXPERT *Essential* Few houses manage to keep back vintage releases, even when years such as 1996 demand it, but this beauty from Paillard, which has

» Single vineyard vs. blends

Blending good champagne is about picking the best
still wines and combining those that work together.
When blending a top wine, a producer is looking for
complexity but not necessarily power. And that's
where the style of single vineyard and blended wines
are different. Complexity in a blend comes from
having different component parts, but a single-
vineyard wine has to come from an exceptional plot
of land, one that has been found to produce
something special. For example, when my great
uncle Pierre Philipponnat bought Clos des Goisses
in 1935 he immediately knew he'd make a single-
vineyard wine from this site.

These champagnes are more about individuality
and power; they're more wine-like. We suggest
decanting Clos des Goisses and not serving it too
cool, at about 54°F, to reveal these facets.

the concentration and structure to deserve such treatment, came onto the market only in 2010. All *grand cru*, the whole batch disgorged in November 2007, it is still very young, quite tight, very fresh with intense citrus spice, like an ice-cold shower to the mouth but with impressive concentration.

Vallée de la Marne

Ayala

Château d'Ay, 2, Boulevard du Nord, 51160 Ay

Tel: +33 (0)3 26 55 15 44
www.champagne-ayala.fr

This previously little-known house was purchased by the Bollinger group in 2005; since the takeover MD Hervé Augustin has set out to raise its profile and draw attention to its well-made wines. He has done this partly by lowering dosage levels across the range, in line with the modern trend among small go-ahead producers, but he has also gone a step further by introducing completely *nondosé* versions of three of the regular cuvées: Brut Majeur nonvintage and Brut Majeur Rosé nonvintage wines and prestige line Perle d'Ayala. Augustin also gives the date of disgorgement on the back labels.

» **Ayala Zéro Dosage NV**
While some companies put together a different blend for their low- or no-dosage champagnes, what is particularly interesting about Ayala is that it uses the same blend as the standard Brut Majeur NV

(which itself has only a low dosage of 8.5 g/l) but no sugar is added at the point of disgorgement. Impressively, the resulting wine is not overly austere. It has good aromatics and shows some finesse and depth, thanks to the quality of the *crus* used and the proportion of reserve wine (which is around 20 percent). In fact, there's a mineral quality that appears to give it more palate texture.

» Perle d'Ayala 2002

EXPERT *Essential* This top-of-the-range wine is made by blending 20 percent Pinot Noir from Aÿ with the Blanc de Blancs vintage cuvée that Ayala produces. This was a dazzling wine itself in 2002, emanating from three *grands crus* Blanc de Blancs vineyards, and its high-quality pedigree shows in this classy, elegant wine, still quite steely in its relative youth after twelve years of aging. Fresh and zesty with some grapefruit notes, it is taut and intense but will open with more time.

Deutz

16, Rue Jeanson, 51160 Aÿ

Tel: +33 (0)3 26 56 94 00
www.champagne-deutz.com

This traditional house built its reputation under the management of five generations of the Lallier-Deutz family prior to a friendly takeover by like-minded quality producer Louis Roederer back in 1993. Since then, with increased investment its fine range of champagnes has hit new heights of excellence. The understated wines, mainly available in the top end of the restaurant trade, are well worth seeking out.

Deutz Brut Classic NV

EXPERT Essential This wine is a fine blueprint for the qualities needed in a top-class non-vintage Champagne. Initially deliciously fresh, it has enough age on release to have developed genuine depth of texture and flavor. The citrus highlights in this lively sherbetty fizz are accompanied by ripe peachy fruit flavors and a fine-grained creamy texture, plus yeasty, savory notes of maturity.

Brut Vintage Rosé 2005

Antique-pink in color, with hints of orange, this satisfyingly ample rosé is wholly made from top-quality Pinot Noir grown on Deutz top vineyard parcels on the south-facing slopes above the village of Ay. The color and some of the depth results from the 10 percent that has been vinified as red wine. This gives it the structure and power to successfully match the fattiness of roast duck or rack of lamb.

Deutz Blanc de Blancs 2004

This is always one of the most dazzling wines in the range, with a sherbetty zip that dances lightly across the tongue, underpinned by a biscuity palate texture—an all-Chardonnay style of real finesse.

Gosset

69, Rue Jules Blondeau, 51160 Ay

Tel: +33 (0)3 26 56 99 56
www.champagne-gosset.com

Gosset, founded in the *grand cru* village of Ay (but recently relocated near Épernay), is the oldest wine house in Champagne, established in 1584. Originally it made mostly table wine, as Ay, along with Beaune, was the main source of red wine for the French court in the sixteenth century. Today it produces full-bodied and richly aromatic champagnes that age particularly well and, because of their affinity with food, are often found on good restaurant wine lists.

» Gosset Grand Rosé Brut NV

An attractive salmon pink, the wine is lifted by a large slug of Chardonnay in the blend (56 percent), while depth comes from red wine sourced from the *grands crus* villages Ambonnay and Bouzy. It has lovely fruit and mouthfeel with a creamy texture but also some zip—a delightful drink.

069

» Gosset Grande Réserve NV Brut

EXPERT *Essential* A three-vintage blend that is aged for five years, Grande Réserve is mostly Chardonnay (43 percent) and Pinot Noir (42 percent) with a dash of Pinot Meunier in the mix to add fruity aromas. It is one of the best nonvintage champagnes on the market, with developed aromas of brioche, vanilla, and ripe stone fruit. Its soft and silky rich palate seduces, and it has an interesting spicy, savory element with a hint of lightly roasted coffee on the finish.

» **Gosset Grand Millésime 2002**

This is made in different vintages than Celebris (see below), but while less expensive it can be very expressive. The blend is a mix of Chardonnay and Pinot Noir that is already quite developed, with rich, warm, spicy notes leading to hints of leather and smoke. It is a big, powerful, characterful champagne that is not for the fainthearted.

» **Celebris Vintage 1998 Extra Brut**

The Celebris trio are all serious wines: vintaged, low dosage, and with a long aging potential. Although made in the classic Gosset style and still youthful, this cuvée has a great intensity of flavor and already shows quite a bit of complexity.

Alfred Gratien

30, Rue Maurice Cerveaux, 51201 Épernay

Tel: +33 (0)3 26 54 38 20 www.alfredgratien.com

This very traditional producer still ferments all of its champagne in small oak casks and makes very expressive, long-lived wines. Although the brand is now owned by a German sparkling wine producer, Henkell & Co., the production methods have not changed, and chef de cave Jean-Paul Jaegar recently passed the baton to his son Nicolas.

» **Brut NV**

EXPERT *Essential* This wine regularly gets four years of aging in the Gratien cellars before release, rather than the more normal two to three that most nonvintage cuvées receive. A pale lemon color, it is quite ripe and rich on the nose, very fresh and lively initially, with good intensity of flavor. This is a top-class fizz that puts many bigger names to shame.

» Brut Vintage 1999

Made from two-thirds Chardonnay, around a quarter Pinot Noir, and 10 percent Pinot Meunier, this is a full-bodied style with great aromatics and length. Already showing some of its hallmark toastiness, it could comfortably age another few years or more—it still needs time to come out of its shell.

» Cuvée Paradis NV

Although it doesn't carry a vintage on the label, this prestige cuvée is actually all produced from a single harvest. The blend majors on Chardonnay (65 percent) with similar amounts of Pinots Noir and

Date of disgorgement

There is a growing movement in Champagne for producers of all types, particularly growers and smaller specialist houses, to put more information on their bottles, such as the exact blend, the harvest base of nonvintage cuvées, the portion of reserve wine, dosage levels, and the date of disgorgement. For consumers, knowing the date of disgorgement allows them to drink the wines when they are young and fresh, within a few months of the disgorgement, or choose to age them longer in their own cellars "on the cork," perhaps several years until they have developed further richness and aromatic complexity.

Meunier. Like the other Gratien wines, it doesn't undergo malolactic fermentation (see page 18), which amplifies the freshness. There are lemon citrus aromas initially with a hint of vanilla, some spiciness, and a honeyed note on the finish.

Jacquesson

68, Rue du Colonel Fabien, 51530 Dizy

Tel: +33 (0)3 26 55 68 11
www.champagnejacquesson.com

This top-class small producer is run by brothers Jean-Hervé and Laurent Chiquet, who have established an enviable reputation for the quality of the Jacquesson wines and all aspects of their operation. The great care they take starts in the vineyard, where they employ traditional methods of viticulture, farming largely organically. Only the cuvée is used and vinification takes place in large oak *foudres*. Uniquely, their nonvintage champagne is not a consistent style but a one-off that changes each year to produce the best possible blend they can make from any individual harvest. These cuvées are now numbered each year upon release—the first from this new philosophy being the 728.

» ### Jacquesson Cuvée 734

Lemon yellow with golden highlights, this champagne has a citrusy streak of acidity, an attractive nutty intensity, and a silky, creamy palate. Already gathering richness, this particular cuvée is noticeably less austere at this stage than some of its predecessors were, though still well short of its peak.These wines mature in much the same way as vintage champagne, gathering complexity as they age.

» Jacquesson 2002 Vintage

EXPERT Essential The last vintage blend made by this house (they are now producing four different single-vineyard vintage champagnes) is a wine to seek out and savor. Opulent and rich on the nose with developed secondary spicy, yeasty notes, it has a balancing acidity, fine palate texture, and expressive minerality. It finishes on a glorious note that seems to last for an eternity—superb.

Alain Thiénot

14, Rue des Moissons, 51100 Reims

Tel: +33 (0)3 26 77 50 10 www.thienot.com

This is a true family business, with Alain Thiénot taking more of a backseat while his son Stanislas and daughter Garance increasingly run the company. They have invested substantially in a new state-of-the-art winery, which was completed in 2003. The estate was built up by Alain based on vineyards in the *grands crus* of Le Mesnil-sur-Oger and Ay and has grown to sixty-seven acres, half of which are *premier* and *grand cru*. The wines are classical and elegant.

» Thiénot Brut Rosé NV

EXPERT Essential At a recent tasting of nonvintage rosé champagnes, this cuvée stood out from the crowd. Made from 45 percent Chardonnay, 28 percent Pinot Noir, 20 percent Pinot Meunier, and the crucial addition of 7 percent red wine from one of the oldest vineyards in Ay, it is a class act with attractive raspberry fruit and a nice refreshing grip of acidity.

» Thiénot Brut NV

A high proportion of Chardonnay helps give this cuvée delicious freshness and finesse. It boasts good concentration and depth, too, partly thanks to a decent proportion of reserve wine. It is very enjoyable and a step up in quality from many more lofty names.

Joseph Perrier

69, Avenue de Paris,
51016 Châlons-en-Champagne

Tel: +33 (0)3 26 68 29 51 www.josephperrier.com

This is the only house making champagne in the agreeable town of Châlons-en-Champagne, several miles east of the main Vallée de la Marne vineyards. Joseph Perrier actually owns vines in the heart of the appellation while it buys in Chardonnay from Avize and Le Mesnil-sur-Oger in the Côte des Blancs. Run by the highly charismatic and hospitable

Jean-Claude Fourmon, whose family is deeply rooted in the region, this fine house produces wines of great charm and serious vintage cuvées.

» Blanc de Blancs Vintage 2002

EXPERT *Essential* A new cuvée of very high quality from this great vintage, where the Chardonnay was the pick of the crop, this wine is a step up in concentration and intensity from the already good nonvintage style. There is plenty of finesse, lovely richness, and impressive length, as you might expect from a champagne sourced from top vineyards in Le Mesnil-sur-Oger, Avize, and Cumières.

» Cuvée Josephine 2002

There was a jump of four years from the rich and forward 1998 vintage to the top-class 2002 for this prestige style, which is a blend of 56 percent Chardonnay and 44 percent Pinot Noir, all sourced from *premiers* and *grands crus* vineyards. Currently, it is taut and fresh, with bright, vivid fruit leading to a rich palate that is dominated by the ripe Chardonnay of this expressive vintage, and a touch of spice on the finish. If true to form, it will go deliciously toasty with age. There is no hurry to drink it up.

» Brut Rosé Vintage 2002

A partner for the Blanc de Blancs vintage, also from the quality 2002 harvest, this classy, fruity, and intense satin-textured rosé is mainly Pinot Noir, freshened with a dash of Chardonnay and made by the addition of 12 percent red wine from Cumières. It has a spicy, toasty character on the finish. Because

» Reserve wine

Nearly all champagne houses that produce non-vintage champagne use reserve wines in their blends — it is entirely legal to make nonvintage champagne all from one harvest but is not usual. Originally reserve wines were used to bring uniformity of style and taste to nonvintage champagne. This is particularly true of the large-volume international brands, which like to preserve a recognizable taste profile, however much of the base harvest changes from year to year.

In addition to promoting regularity of style, among quality-minded producers reserve wine is also increasingly employed to add nuances of flavor, complexity, and finesse, and to provide character and distinctiveness. It may be overstating the case to claim that nonvintage champagnes with a large proportion of reserve wines in them are necessarily better, but it is certainly true to say that with higher proportions of reserve wine you are likely to find greater complexity and more interesting wine.

Joseph Perrier is not as widely renowned as the quality of its wines deserve, it is also priced attractively at a similar level to some top-rated nonvintage rosés.

Philipponnat

13, Rue du Pont, 51160 Mareuil-sur-Ay

Tel: +33 (0)3 26 56 93 01 www.philipponnat.com

The quality across the whole Pinot Noir–dominated range at Philipponnat has improved impressively over the past nine years under Charles Philipponnat's skillful management, particularly the nonvintage Royale Réserve. Better use is being made of the 49.4 acres of vines that the company owns in some of the best *crus* on the southern slopes of the Montagne de Reims. The jewel in its crown remains Clos des Goisses, a steep 13.6-acre, south-facing vineyard on pure chalky soils, which produces some of the ripest and richest wine in the whole of Champagne.

» **Royale Réserve Brut NV**
Elegant and biscuity with a creamy richness and good texture in the mouth, this has become one of the best nonvintage champagnes in the appellation. Complexity is added by quite a high portion of reserve wine and the fact that these reserves from previous harvests are now kept in oak barrels.

» **Cuvée 1522 Millésime 2000**
This wine, a rich and pure 60/40 Pinot Noir-Chardonnay blend, commemorates the first historical record of the Philipponnat family in the village of Mareuil-sur-Ay. Already quite rich and

toasty with generosity of flavor and aroma, this vintage has elegance, too, but hasn't yet reached its peak.

›› Clos des Goisses 1998

EXPERT Essential This Clos des Goisses vintage was released a year after the 1999 vintage, because, as Charles Philipponnat says, it is a massive, deeply structured wine of great intensity that needed more time for its diverse elements to integrate better. According to Philipponnat it has the potential to age for decades, not just a few more years, and there is evidence in the bottle—great structure and concentration—to support this viewpoint.

Côte des Bar

Drappier

Rue des Vignes, 10200 Urville

Tel: +33 (0)3 25 27 40 15
www.champagne-drappier.com

Michel Drappier makes a fine selection of mostly Pinot Noir–based, characterful, expressive wines, some of which hint at the close physical proximity of Burgundy. He has even devised a special decanter to help intensify the powerful vinous aromas. The range includes a fine, mineral all-Pinot Noir Brut Nature champagne, mainly sold in French restaurants, plus an innovative four-varietal Blanc de Blancs blend (Cuvée Quattuor) of Chardonnay, Pinot Blanc, and rarities Arbane and Petit Meslier.

» Val des Demoiselles Brut Rosé NV

This wine looks almost like a light Burgundian red, with ripe, delicious Pinot Noir fruit dominating the palate. It is made by the *saignée* method and the resulting concentration of red fruit is so strong that Michel Drappier lightens it slightly by the addition of a little Pinot Noir vinified as white wine. The final color of the wine varies depending on which harvest it is based. This is one of the very best nonvintage rosés around and not at all expensive.

» Cuvée Millésime Exception 2002

The 2002 vintage in champagne is arguably the most consistently good year for over a decade. Nearly all the wines have looked attractive at release while also showing good aging potential. This Drappier vintage is another fine example of the genre, at once ample, forward, rich, and beautifully balanced. While it is highly enjoyable now, with a few years of extra cellaring, it will develop greater complexity.

» Grande Sendrée Vintage 2002

EXPERT *Essential* Produced from a steep south-facing site in Urville, this blend of 45 percent Chardonnay and 55 percent Pinot Noir is the prestige cuvée of the house and the star of the range. Silky-textured, rich, but beautifully balanced, it has more than a whiff of Burgundy about it, as well as floral notes and aromas of mandarin, soft spices, and honey.

>> **Brut Nature**

This *non dosé*, 100 percent Pinot Noir champagne was first launched in 1999. Clean, fresh, with a salty, mineral, almost iodine note, it makes a fine palate-cleansing aperitif or accompaniment to oysters.

Côte des Blancs

Champagne Veuve Fourny et Fils

12-5, Rue du Mesnil, 51130 Vertus

Tel: +33 (0)3 26 52 16 30
www.champagne-veuve-fourny.com

Emmanuel and Charles-Henry Fourny run this family business scrupulously—and with great attention to detail. Their reputation for producing pure, refined, long-lived, low- and zero-dosage wines is definitely in the ascendance. They farm some thirty-seven acres of vineyards with forty separate parcels of land, all located within the highly rated *premier cru* of Vertus, mostly planted with Chardonnay on three different soil types.

>> **Cuvée R Extra Brut NV**

EXPERT *Essential* Named after the brothers' father, Roger Fourny, this superb wine is made with a majority of Chardonnay and a *soupçon* of Pinot Noir. Vinified in small oak casks, it comes from organically grown vines that are an average age of forty-three years old and produce a concentrated, richly aromatic juice. It is made from a high-quality base. Elegant and energetic, it has initial aromas of white flower and fresh citrus fruits. On the palate there is a distinct saline note, and savory, complex, smoky, yeasty flavors evolve while a streak of mineral purity is maintained in the long, rich finish.

>> **Clos des Faubourgs de Notre Dame 1999**
Emanating from a tiny walled single-vineyard plot of about half an acre, replanted in 1951, this all-Chardonnay cuvée has more color and intensity and some fatness in the mouth, plus a marked chalky minerality. Only a few hundred bottles are made each vintage of this long-lived classy fizz that will develop more creaminess as it ages.

Salon and Delamotte

5-7 Rue de la Brèche d'Oger,
51190 Le Mesnil-sur-Oger

Tel: +33 (0)3 26 57 51 65
www.salondelamotte.com

These two houses, both owned by the Laurent-Perrier group, share premises in Le Mesnil-sur-Oger. Salon is unusual in producing just one cuvée, all from Le Mesnil fruit, and not every harvest. Its fine, extremely long-lived Blanc de Blancs style is always vintaged and only made in the best years. The Delamotte cuvées benefit as they take the Le Mesnil fruit in the many years that Salon is not made.

>> **Salon 1997**
In their youth (which may last a dozen years or more) these wines are often unapproachably steely and quite impenetrable, even unattractive. They really need time to show complexity in addition to the core of pure, saline elegance.

» Growers

Growing individuality

Only about half of the growers that make and sell champagne under their own labels export it to markets outside France, and they account for no more than 5 percent of total champagne exports. There is a growing band of artisan producers that make small volumes of individual and characterful wine that reflects the specific *terroir*—often just one *cru* or village in the region—on which it is produced. Interest in these champagnes is developing rapidly, partly in reaction to the uniformity of some of the big brands. This is where to find much of the current vinous excitement in the region, while the wines offer a particularly good quality-to-price ratio.

West and southwest of Reims

Chartogne-Taillet

37, Grand-Rue, 51220 Merfy

Tel: +33 (0)3 26 03 10 17
www.chartogne-taillet.com

This quality grower-producer, based in the sleepy village of Merfy, is now run by Alexandre Chartogne-Taillet, who took over from his parents in 2006. While the family's reputation for its wines was already established, he has brought in new ideas both about organic farming (ending herbicide and pesticide use, plowing between the vines by horse) and how the wines are made. In recent years he has lowered sulfur and dosage levels and introduced some oak, for example.

›› Millésime 2002 Brut

This poised 50/50 Pinot Noir-Chardonnay blend from the exceptional 2002 harvest is satisfyingly Pinot-rich, with meaty, savory notes, a yeasty, chewy palate texture plus a hint of minerality and spiciness. The dosage is low at 7 g/l.

›› Cuvée Sainte Anne Brut NV

This wine, a 60 percent Chardonnay, 40 percent Pinot Noir, is blended with 20 percent reserve wine. It is unfiltered and unfined, and the dosage is low enough (at 4.5 g/l) to make it an extra brut style, which helps preserve vivacity. With notes of freshly baked pastries, it also has an attractive ripe peach fruit element and good length.

›› Cuvée Fiacre "Tête de Cuvée"

Fiacre is Chartogne-Taillet's prestige cuvée and, although unvintaged on the label, comes from a single harvest, 2006 in this case. Made from a 60 percent Chardonnay, 40 percent Pinot Noir blend, this is an ample, complex, and expressive wine with impressive concentration and a long finish.

Jérôme Prévost

2, Rue Petite Montagne, 51390 Gueux

Tel: +33 (0)3 26 03 48 60

Jérôme Prévost's tiny production of some thirteen thousand bottles of oak-fermented, Pinot Meunier-based champagne is much sought after. He makes one main wine, plus a tiny production of rosé, from five acres of biodynamically farmed forty-year-old Pinot Meunier, though he also has an additional half-acre plot planted with young vines of other varieties. As well as fermenting in oak, the wines are all made with natural yeasts, without fining or filtering and using as little sulfur as possible. No dosage is added on disgorgement.

» La Closerie Les Béguines Brut Nature

EXPERT *Essential* This wine, which is made entirely from a single harvest with no reserve wine accounts for the majority of production. Powerful, lively, and intensely expressive, it is outside most people's experience of champagne. It is very vinous, with developed, yeasty, smoky aromas that follow through in the rich palate and a long and complex finish.

Champagne Maillart

5, Rue de Villers aux Noeuds, 51500 Ecueil

Tel: +33 (0)3 26 49 77 89
www.champagne-maillart.fr

Nicolas Maillart is another young winemaker who has revolutionized the way he makes wine. He now widely uses oak fermentation, experimenting with locally produced barrels, has generally reduced dosage levels, and has increased the reserve wine element in his blends.

» Maillart Brut Rosé Grand Cru NV (Bouzy)

This is a blend of 70 percent Pinot Noir and 30 percent Chardonnay, with an attractive salmon-pink color extracted by maceration from the skins of the black grapes. A portion of oak-fermented wine in the blend adds complexity; a light dosage of 6 g/l keeps the style fresh and elegant. With notes of ripe fruits and a vanilla element coming partly from the oak, the wine is suffused with the powerful Bouzy fruit.

» Les Franc de Pieds 2003 Extra Brut Premier Cru

EXPERT Essential Made only in the best vintages, this wine comes from a south-facing, small ungrafted Pinot Noir vineyard in Écueil, planted in 1973. It is fermented and aged in oak vats with *batonnage* (lees stirring), while the malolactic fermentation is blocked to help preserve freshness. It is bottled unfiltered with virtually no dosage (just 2 g/l). Golden-hued with intense ripe fruit aromas, hints of almond, and a rich caramel note, it is a pure and expressive *terroir*-driven wine.

Premier Cru Brut NV Platine

This assemblage of 80 percent Pinot Noir and 20 percent Chardonnay has between 30 and 40 percent reserve wine (depending on the harvest) that has been aged in oak in the blend, and this helps allow a relatively low dosage of 7 g/l. With a fine mousse of persistent small bubbles, it is full of life, with a taut, clean, fresh, lifted style, some grapefruit citrus notes, good intensity, and a long clean finish.

Bérèche et Fils

Le Craon de Ludes, 51500 Ludes

Tel: +33 (0)3 26 61 13 28
www.champagne-bereche-et-fils.com

The Bérèche family has twenty-three acres of vineyard in six different *crus*, mostly in what is known as the Petite Montagne de Reims. The family treats its soils with respect, eschewing chemical treatments, using horses to plow between vines, and gradually increasing the proportion farmed biodynamically. Yields are generally kept much lower than the average in Champagne, with an annual production of around eighty-five thousand bottles. Bérèche et Fils takes a noninterventional approach to winemaking, using natural yeasts for the initial ferments, which partly take place in oak, without any malolactic fermentation or filtering, and low dosage levels.

Extra Brut Réserve NV

The purity of flavors in the Bérèche wines is particularly noticeable in this extra brut style that has just a 2 g/l dosage, giving a nicely defined mineral touch, fine mouth texture with dried fruit notes and a hint of bitterness on the finish. Like the brut style, this is a three-way blend of Chardonnay, Pinot Meunier, and Pinot Noir, which is 15 percent oak-fermented with 30 percent reserve wine from the two previous harvests, but it gets a year's extra aging before release.

» Reflet d'Antan

The most expensive Bérèche wine is matured in barrels for nearly a year following some eighteen months of aging on fine lees in tanks and has been produced since 1985 under the Bérèche version of the "solera system" (see page 90). The current blend on the market has a small element of reserve wine that dates back over twenty-five years. Although extra brut in style (6 g/l dosage), this wine—and it is more wine than champagne—is full-bodied, rich, complex, and evolved, with pronounced yeasty aromas and a very creamy palate, plus a savory note on the finish.

089

Dehours & Fils

2, Rue de la Chapelle, 51700 Cerseuil

Tel: +33 (0)3 26 52 71 75
www.champagne-dehours.fr

Fourth-generation independent grower Jérôme Dehours and his brother-in-law Jean-Marc Laisne produce a fine range of champagnes from their numerous parcels of vines split between Mareuil-le-Port, Oeuilly, and Troissy. Dehours uses a *perpétuelle réserve* (see page 90) first set up in 1998 for his five white nonvintage blends with Trio "S" Brut, a three-varietal blend that comes entirely from this solera system. He also makes two single-vineyard, vintage

>> ## The solera system

Some champagne wine reserves are run in a way
that is similar to the solera system used in the
production of sherry. At its simplest this might
involve combining the nonvintage cuvée blend with
a certain amount (10 to 20 percent) of the previous
year's nonvintage release, which is kept back for this
purpose. This adds nuances of complexity to the new
cuvée, and each succeeding year this base wine will
gradually contain more and older component parts.
Bruno Paillard's and Philipponnat's main nonvintage cuvées both employ such a system.

Other producers have taken the idea a stage further
and developed what is called a *réserve perpétuelle*,
involving a number of barrels. For each nonvintage
cuvée produced, a certain amount of reserve wine
(perhaps a third of the blend) is taken from the last
barrel and combined with the new harvest. A portion
of this new nonvintage blend is used each year to top
up the first barrel in the solera.

champagnes: one a Blanc de Noirs, the other a three-way blend from two parcels of land in Mareuil-le-Port.

» La Côte en Bosses 2004 Mareuil-le-Port Extra Brut

An extraordinary blend of all three main grape varieties from old vines fermented in small oak *barriques*, this is the sort of wine that is drawing attention to a small band of quality-champagne growers pushing the boundaries. Just 2,681 bottles were produced in 2004, and they were disgorged in 2010, in an extra brut style with just 4 g/l dosage. This is a complex, developed wine of real palate weight and intensity that remains lively and vigorous.

» Maisoncelle 2004 Mareuil-le-Port Extra Brut

This wine comes from a very small parcel of old vines of Pinot Noir with a minute amount of ungrafted Meunier. Just 3,047 bottles were made in 2004. It was disgorged in 2010 with a dosage of just 3 g/l. Fresh and even citrusy initially, it has a noticeable saline, mineral quality and a savory intensity that makes it stand out from the crowd.

Montagne de Reims

Vilmart & Cie

5, Rue des Gravières, 51500 Rilly-la-Montagne

Tel: +33 (0)3 26 03 40 01
www.champagnevilmart.fr

In the early 1990s, Vilmart was one of the first grower-producers to establish a reputation outside

France for its wines, which now command quite serious prices. Based in the pretty and quiet backwater of Rilly-la-Montagne on the northern slopes of the Montagne de Reims, and run by Laurent Champs, it owns twenty-seven acres of *premiers crus* vineyards mostly planted with Chardonnay (60 percent) and Pinot Noir (37 percent) as well as 3 percent Meunier, which are farmed largely organically.

» **Grand Cellier Brut NV**

While Grand Reserve is 70 percent Pinot Noir, the Chardonnay-dominant (70 percent) Grand Cellier, which is aged a year longer, is more expressive. A lifted, energetic fizz with a pronounced spiciness, it also has a developed, quite exotic, fruity richness and shows impressive concentration.

093

» **Coeur de Cuvée 2004**

EXPERT *Essential* This wine is 80 percent Chardonnay and 20 percent Pinot Noir, made and aged in new and one-year-old *barriques*, though the oak seems restrained. It comes from the fifty-year-old vineyard Blanche Voies, and this shows in greater freshness, more finesse and a noticeably long finish, though it will develop more with extra aging.

Paul Déthune

2, Rue du Moulin, 51150 Ambonnay

Tel: +33 (0)3 26 57 01 88
www.champagne-dethune.com

Pierre and Sophie Déthune produce an attractive range of wines from the 17.3-acre vineyard they farm sustainably. While stainless-steel fermentation has become the norm in Champagne, many new-generation growers are returning to either total or partial oak fermenting and aging with good results. The Déthune wines are a good example of this and beautifully express the ampleness and richness of Ambonnay fruit.

» **Grand Cru Blancs de Noirs**

Although it isn't declared as a vintage, this wine is typically all from a single harvest and is both fermented and aged in used oak barrels. Rich and rounded, but not at all heavy, it shows an attractive honeyed, beeswax note along with a nice depth of red-berry fruit.

» **Brut Prestige**

This is a 50/50 blend of Chardonnay and Pinot Noir, made with 25 percent reserve wines. The nose is developed, with aromas of toasted bread and dried fruit, while the palate texture is seductively soft and creamy, thanks to the Chardonnay, with notes of vanilla and a spicy, gingerbread element.

Rodez

4, Rue de Isse, 51150 Ambonnay

Tel: +33 (0)3 26 57 04 93
www.champagne-rodez.fr

After working with other vignerons, Eric Rodez returned to the family domain in 1982 and set about introducing changes based on his experiences. His sixteen acres of vineyard in the *grand cru* of Ambonnay are farmed with minimal chemical treatments. Planted with 55 percent Pinot Noir and 45 percent Chardonnay, all thirty-five parcels are vinified separately, giving a wide range of blending options.

» ### Rodez Cuvée des Crayères Brut NV
This is a six-harvest blend, based mostly on 2008, but also on 2007 and 2006, with additional small splashes

Crémant style

To get champagne, or any sparkling wine, to re-ferment for a second time in the bottle (to create bubbles) a certain amount of yeast, yeast nutrients, and sugar are added to the final blend of still wine. The amount of sugar depends on the degree of effervescence required. Most champagne is fully *mousseux*, that is to say a sparkling wine with a pressure of 5 to 6 atmospheres. There are, however, a few champagnes deliberately made in a *crémant* style (such as Mumm de Cramant) at a slightly lower pressure (3.6 atmospheres), and these tend to taste slightly softer, creamier, and are less fizzy.

of 2005, 2004, and 2002 (with equal parts Chardonnay and Pinot Noir). It has an attractive, developed style with floral notes and some honeyed richness.

>> **Rodez 2000 Millésime**
A 50/50 Pinot Noir-Chardonnay blend, with 80 percent vinified in oak, this has a lovely rich golden color and is surprisingly fresh with a clean, bright finish, while the well-integrated oak plays only a supporting role.

>> **Rodez Grand Vintages**
This is a complex blend of diminishing portions of the best recent vintages, seven in this case (2004, 2002, 2000, 1999, 1998, 1996, 1995), all vinified in oak. A rich, vinous style, it has a lovely silky texture but retains a decent freshness, too.

Roger Brun

10, Rue St Vincent, 51160 Ay

Tel: +33 (0)3 26 55 45 50
www.champagne-roger-brun.com

Located in the center of an important *grand cru* village, this fine grower-producer is now run by the friendly and charismatic Philippe Brun, who operates one of the main presses. Brun makes an excellent range of characterful champagnes, using the family vineyards, which are mainly located in Ay.

>> **Ay Grand Cru Brut NV**
A Blanc de Noirs from the *grand cru* of Ay, this is a wine of structure and finesse, with a freshness and purity of fruit in its youth that shows its pedigree and encourages the extra cellaring it will benefit

from, developing more richness and complexity over time.

» **Cuvée des Sires 99/00**

This is one of Brun's top cuvées, a blend of Ay Pinot Noir (around 70 percent) and Chardonnay from some of his best plots of vineyard. It is vinified in old oak barrels and has a low dosage of 8 g/l. On first release (typically after at least five years of aging in bottle on its lees) it remains youthfully fresh, with notes of lemon citrus and honey. With several years of additional aging, it becomes deliciously toasty. This is serious champagne to be savored and enjoyed at your leisure.

» **Cuvée des Sires La Pelle 2002**

EXPERT *Essential* This sublime wine is made only in the very best vintages and comes from a tiny 1.63-acre plot near the cemetery in Ay. It is partly vinified in oak barrels and has a low dosage of just 3 g/l. Ripe, rich, and powerfully structured with a noticeable mineral element, this is a deliciously complex wine with a pronounced buttery creaminess and great length.

Vallée de la Marne

René Geoffroy

4, Rue Jeanson, 51160 Ay

Tel: +33 (0)3 26 55 32 31
www.champagne-geoffroy.com

Formerly based in the top *premier cru* village of Cumières, where the family's 34.6 acres of vineyards are located, Jean-Baptiste Geoffroy now has a brand-new winery in nearby Aÿ. This passionate winemaker is excited about the quality of juice he gets here from two reconditioned traditional presses, a gravity-fed system that allows minimal handling and has the space to keep small parcels of wine separately, which increases his blending options.

>> **Cuvée Empreinte NV**

The blend for this wine varies from harvest to harvest, but it is mainly Pinot Noir, with at least half (sometimes all) vinified in large oak *foudres* to help develop complexity and the evolution of the wine. Mellow, ripe, and rich on the nose, it retains a nice zippy edge, thanks partly to the low dosage of 6–7 g/l.

>> **Volupté Tête de Cuvée**

From some of the family's oldest vineyards in Cumières, this is usually a Chardonnay and Pinot Noir blend. In 2005 the cuvée was 100 percent Chardonnay—50 percent fermented in large oak *foudres*, the other half in *barriques*. The first sensation is of full and ripe fruit, but there is an underlying brisk acidity and a fresh finish.

>> **Millésime 2000 Extra Brut**

Again, Chardonnay is dominant in this extra brut blend, which has just 2 g/l dosage. A bright, light gold in color, this was a ripe harvest; it is 100 percent fermented in used Burgundian oak barrels. Reticent at first, this cuvée needs time to open up in the glass, revealing a full and rich palate, a chalky mineral note, and an impressively long finish.

Bruno Michel

4, Allée de la Vieille Ferme, 51530 Pierry

Tel: +33 (0)3 26 55 10 54

Grower Bruno Michel is a Pinot Meunier specialist, just like his father, José Michel, who was famous for his collection of older vintages, though Bruno also has some Chardonnay and Pinot Noir vineyards. He farms some thirty-seven acres, mainly organically. His wines are partly vinified in oak (the vintage cuvées are wholly fermented in oak) and partly in stainless steel; his reserve wines are also kept in oak.

» Cuvée Blanche

This entry-level wine is a blend of 50 percent Chardonnay and 50 percent Pinot Meunier, based on the 2004 harvest, with 30 percent reserve wine from 2003. It is mellow, soft, and rounded while really fresh and energetic, a style that makes for very enjoyable drinking.

» Premier Cru Blanc de Blancs NV Brut

An attractive wine combining freshness, richness, and complexity, this is made from even amounts of the 2003 and 2004 harvests, which is vinified in oak and stays in wood for ten months prior to bottling. It is surprisingly fresh in spite of the oak fermentation but with an attractive richness in the mouth and some spiciness.

» Cuvée Special 2000

EXPERT Essential Made 100 percent from Pinot Meunier, aged one year in oak, this cuvée gives off aromas of the forest floor after rain and has a distinctive mushroom truffly note. It is a very vinous expression of champagne that comes from Bruno's best fifty-year-old Pinot Meunier vines.

» "Les Rosés"

This single-vineyard *saignée* rosé comes from a specific plot of forty-five-year-old vines in Saint-Agnan near Dormans. It is a wine of real character and complexity, with exotic aromas of ripe mango, a spicy element, and a deliciously creamy texture.

Côte des Blancs

Agrapart & Fils

57, Avenue Jean Jaures, 51190 Avize

Tel: +33 (0)3 26 57 51 38
www.champagne-agrapart.com

Pascal and Fabrice Agrapart own twenty-four acres of prime vineyard, the majority in the *grands crus* villages of Avize, Oger, Cramant, and Oiry, divided into sixty-two separate plots. These plots are all vinified separately in oak, making use of natural yeasts, with minimal intervention. No chemical pesticides or weed killers are used, the vineyards are plowed, and the wines are never chaptalized.

» Les 7 Crus

A two-vintage blend of four *grands crus* and three *premiers crus*. The dosage is just 7 g/l. A quarter is aged in large old oak *demi-muids* (a barrel that holds 600 liters/159 gallons), the rest in stainless steel. The result is a gentle, harmonious

» Vintage value

The majority of champagne sales are nonvintage,
but then there is a leap to much more expensive
prestige cuvées while the vintage sector tends to get
forgotten. But vintage often offers quality for far less
money. You get a beautiful representation of house
style, slightly different vintage to vintage because it is
all from a single year. The wines are mostly quite
mature when first sold but will often age further
attractively. At the moment there are some very fine
years available, such as 2002, plus some 1990s that
also impress, such as Gosset and Pol Roger Blanc de
Blancs, which is an exceptional wine. Outside of
sherry there isn't another sector of the fine wine
market where older vintages are so readily available.

They are also terrific value: while prestige cuvées
are mainly over $150, there is a selection of top
vintages between $70 and $115, for example, Joseph
Perrier's Blanc de Blancs and vintage rosé, both from
2002, are under $92 a bottle.

nonvintage cuvée with creamy notes and a fine, taut minerality.

Franck Bonville

9, Rue Pasteur, 51190 Avize

Tel: +33 (0)3 26 57 52 30
www.champagne-franck-bonville.com

Established by Franck Bonville in 1937, this family business is now run by his son Gilles and grandson Olivier, who is the winemaker. He has 44.5 acres of prime vineyard in the *grands crus* of Cramant, Avize, and Oger. His aim is to express the freshness and mineral qualities of this chalky *terroir*.

» **Brut Blanc de Blancs Grand Cru**

This is an excitingly fresh, lifted, and mineral Blanc de Blancs style, with reserve wine giving it extra depth, length, and complexity. It is all made from *grand cru* Chardonnay. The current cuvée is from a harvest base of 2010 (70 percent) with 30 percent reserve wine and a dosage of 9.5 g/l.

» **Les Belles Voyes**

This cuvée is vinified (and aged for seven months) in oak and produced from the best vineyard parcels in Oger. The oak adds a vinous gloss of richness and an extra layer of complexity, making this a particularly food-friendly wine.

›› **Millésime 2007 Grand Cru Blanc de Blancs Brut**

EXPERT *Essential* A blend of two *grand cru* terroirs, Avize and Oger, this lovely champagne is fresh and lifted with a soft cushion of tiny bubbles that give it a beautiful creamy texture in the mouth. It has a quite developed biscuity note, great balance, and a polished finish that leaves you wanting more.

Claude Cazals

28, Rue du Grand Mont,
51190 Le Mesnil-sur-Oger

Tel: +33 (0) 3 26 57 52 26
www.champagne-claude-cazals.net

This family business in Le Mesnil-sur-Oger is run by Delphine Cazals (who is married to Olivier Bonville of Franck Bonville in Avize) and has 22.2 acres of *grands* and *premiers crus* vineyards in the Côte des Blancs. This includes a nine-acre walled *clos* in Oger, where the oldest vines, planted in the 1950s, have been used each year since 1995 to make the single-vineyard Le Clos Cazals.

⟫ Le Clos Cazals 1998

EXPERT *Essential* The grapes in the beautifully situated *clos* regularly attain an extra degree of maturity thanks to the shelter afforded by the walls and the aspect of the vines. The 1998 vintage was a golden-colored, lusciously rich, silken textured, honeyed wine of pure hedonistic drinking pleasure—burnished sunshine in a glass with the richness and mouthfeel of top Meursault, plus terrific length. Only four thousand bottles and two hundred magnums are made each year.

» **Cuvée Vive Grand Cru Extra Brut NV**
A lovely light-gold hue, this wine exudes ripe, stone-fruit aromas of quince with a note of honey. While it has good fresh acidity, the emphasis is on generous fruit ripeness, belying the cuvée's low dosage. There is a buttery note and some biscuit mouthfeel, and just a note of minerality on the finish.

Pierre Gimonnet & Fils

1, Rue de la République, 51530 Cuis

Tel: +33 (0)3 26 59 78 70
www.champagne-gimonnet.com

The Blanc de Blancs champagnes made by brothers Didier and Olivier Gimonnet are exemplary Côte des Blancs Chardonnays: taut, intense, mineral-edged wines of finesse and elegance. The brothers make good use of their 64.2 acres of vineyard: half are in the *grands crus* villages of Cramant and Chouilly, the rest in the highly regarded *premier cru* of Cuis.

» **Gimonnet Cuis Premier Cru Brut NV**
This cuvée has a harvest base of 2009 with reserve wines from 2007, 2006, and 2004, themselves assemblages with older component parts, which adds complexity. It has a light dosage of just 8 g/l. Brisk and zesty with a lifted grapefruit zing to it, this champagne is a great, refreshing pick-me-up, but also has some chalky minerality. It seems to get more impressive year after year.

Brut Gastronome 2004

EXPERT *Essential* A blend of Chardonnays from Chouilly (49 percent), Cuis (39.8 percent), and Cramant (11.2 percent) makes this wine brilliantly lively. It also has some spiciness and a lovely developed palate texture and mouthfeel—a class act.

Champagne André Jacquart

63, Avenue de Bammental, 51130 Vertus

Tel: +33 (0)3 26 57 52 29
www.couleursdoyard.com

In 2004, a dynamic new generation took over this grower that boasts a 59.3-acre estate. Brother and sister Benoit and Marie Doyard built a completely new winery and now produce just four champagnes using the best fruit from their *premiers* and *grands*

105

Sweet to dry

As recently as the mid-nineteenth century all champagne was made in a sweet style. These days dosage levels in most commercial champagnes have come down on average. "Doux" is the sweetest, with a dosage level above 50 g/l, but very little is made, while in the 1850s there were many wines with more than twice that. The move toward "brut" styles began in the 1870s, but it was over a century before any sizeable house, Laurent-Perrier in this case, launched a zero-dosage champagne in the shape of Ultra Brut, in 1981.

crus vineyards in Vertus and Le Mesnil-sur-Oger. They have halved their annual production, down to around eighty thousand bottles, in the search for quality. Their new Experience range was launched in January 2008—all the wines undergo some oak fermentation, dosage levels have been reduced to a very low 3 g/l, and each bears a date of disgorgement.

» Brut Experience Premier Cru NV

Made from a blend of *premier* and *grand cru* Chardonnay, this wine is part oak-fermented but does not undergo malolactic fermentation, thus preserving its exhilarating freshness. It is concentrated, mineral, lifted, and more accessible in its youth than its counterpart Mesnil Grand Cru Brut.

» Mesnil Experience Grand Cru Brut NV

EXPERT *Essential* This impressive fizz is based on the 2004 harvest with around 10 percent reserve wine. Eighty percent of it is barrel-fermented, but such treatment barely tames the Mesnil fruit; the wine remained quite linear and steely on initial release but with recognizable concentration and mineral power. Now, after additional years of aging, it has blossomed into something richer, more complex, and aromatically expressive, with toasty, smoky notes and a long evolved finish.

Larmandier-Bernier

19, Avenue du Général de Gaulle, 51130 Vertus

Tel: +33 (0)3 26 52 13 24 www.larmandier.fr

Arguably the most respected and admired grower-producer in the whole of Champagne, Pierre

Larmandier remains self-effacingly modest, although his wines have achieved critical acclaim worldwide. His vineyards are farmed biodynamically, and he uses oak barrels and large oak *foudres* to ferment much of the base wine and to store reserves. His winemaking and attention to detail are meticulous, and the wines are stunning across the range.

» Tradition Premier Cru Vertus NV

A blend of 85 percent Chardonnay and 15 percent Pinot Noir (a little less Pinot Noir than in the past), this wine is based on the harvest of 2007, with 30 percent reserve wine stored in casks and oak vats in a kind of solera system (the oldest from the 2002 harvest). With a ripe, full nose and purity of fruit, it has a low dosage at just 4 g/l, but it is still rich and keeps minerality, with a salty note on the tongue.

» Terre de Vertus Premier Cru (non-dosé)

EXPERT *Essential* This wine comes from two parcels of a mid-slope vineyard in Vertus, the individual qualities of which Pierre discovered in blind tastings. Lemon yellow with gold highlights, explosively fresh but rich in the mouth, it has ripe developed aromas, with a very noticeable biscuit texture. It is impressively powerful and complex, with a very long finish.

» Blanc de Blancs Premier Cru
Vertus NV Extra Brut

This has a different nose—not the roundness and richness of the blend, but ripe fruit and an early spicy note. There is good freshness, but the emphasis is on the minerality. It has a quite developed creamy palate feel and biscuity mouth texture, some honeyed notes, and a long finish. With more time it will develop further complexity. Made from a 2007 harvest base, the Vertus Chardonnay component comes from the chalkier northern part of the *cru* and is blended with *grand cru* Chardonnay from Cramant and Oger and a large portion of reserve wine.

» Rosé de Saignée Premier Cru (Vertus)

Presented in a frosted bottle, this is made entirely from the 2009 harvest and so could be vintage. A light ruby-red color, achieved by two to three days' maceration, it has aromas of red fruits and is made in a very clean and fresh style. The initial red fruits evolve into black fruits in the mouth.

» Vielles Vignes de Cramant Grand Cru 2005

Less obvious or open on the nose initially, this wine nonetheless has a very developed rich palate and a luxuriant creamy texture with distinctive biscuity notes. It has almost no dosage at just 2 g/l, but is a complex wine of real intensity and richness that changes constantly in the glass, gradually revealing more complexity.

» Cooperatives

Developing investments

Less than a quarter of the cooperatives operating in Champagne actually sell the finished product; between them they account for just 10 percent of worldwide champagne sales. However, aware of the need to be competitive, and in an effort to sell more wines at a higher price level to boost the income of their grape growers, the top co-ops have invested heavily in the latest equipment over the past couple of decades and some now make serious-quality champagne. Several have always had good access to the best grapes through the *grands crus* and *premiers crus* vineyards owned by their grower members, and now they have the technical know-how and winemaking kit to take full advantage of this.

Reims

De Castelnau

5, Rue Gosset, 51066 Reims

Tel: +33 (0)3 26 77 89 00
www.champagne-de-castelnau.eu

The De Castelnau brand is produced by the Coopérative Régionale des Vins de Champagne of Reims (CRVC), which has some 640 grower-members, who own 2,038 acres of vineyard, more than half in *premiers* and *grands crus*. As well as being able to source grapes from these top vineyards the CRVC boasts one of the best respected winemakers in Champagne, Richard Dailly, who has been working with this co-op for nearly twenty years and is a highly skilled blender.

» De Castelnau Brut NV

Thanks to extra aging (typically four years before release) and the extensive use of reserve wines, adding depth and complexity, this cuvée has an attractive, soft-textured, and quite developed rich style.

» De Castelnau Cuvée Spéciale Millésime 2002

This is the first vintage of this cuvée, which has a higher proportion of Chardonnay (61 percent) in the blend than De Castelnau's regular vintage offering; it benefits from the high quality of 2002 Chardonnay, which gives the wine an attractive and buttery richness with aromas of white peach and a honeyed note, plus good length.

» De Castelnau Brut Rosé NV

EXPERT *Essential* This wine is decently fruity and made in a soft creamy style. It is one of the most enjoyably drinkable non-vintage pink fizzes on the market and great value for money.

Jacquart

34, Boulevard Lundy, 51100 Reims

Tel: +33 (0)3 26 07 88 40
www.champagne-jacquart.fr

The Jacquart brand is produced by Alliance Champagne which is co-owned by three different cooperative groups that are spread across the region; one in Château Thierry to the western edge of the appellation nearest Paris, another is located fairly centrally in Ay, while the third is in the southernmost Côte des Bar vineyard near Troyes. With its members owning 5,683 acres of vineyard spread across the appellation, Alliance has lots of blending options for the production of the Jacquart range.

» Jacquart Brut de Nominée NV

EXPERT *Essential* This is the cognoscenti's pick of the range, a roughly 50/50 Chardonnay and Pinot Noir blend with a lovely balance and bright citrus highlights. It develops a sumptuous richness over time but retains good refreshing acidity, too.

» Jacquart Brut Grand Millésime 2000

This opulent, toasty, and nicely mature blend of 55 percent Pinot Noir, 45 percent Chardonnay is available now only under the Jacquart Oenothèque range, but it is worth seeking out, especially in magnum, where the freshness is accentuated.

Montagne de Reims

Mailly Grand Cru

28, Rue de la Libération, 51500 Mailly

Tel: +33 (0)3 26 49 41 10
www.champagne-mailly.com

The Grand Cru cooperative at Mailly in the Montagne de Reims is a good example of how the best cooperatives have invested significantly in upgrading their wineries over the past decade or so. Owned by seventy-seven growers from twenty-five families, this co-op boasts 173 acres of prime *grand cru* vineyard all around Mailly, three-quarters of it planted with Pinot Noir, the rest with Chardonnay. It produces mainly rich, full-bodied Pinot Noir-led wines, of great intensity and vigor that need time to mellow and show at their best.

» **Extra Brut**

This cuvée, a three-way blend of 2005, 2004, and 2003 harvests, has no dosage and really needs the additional aging time it gets before release. Even after five years of maturing it is still very lively and fresh, with a noticeable mineral note and a long, fine linear finish.

» **Les Enchansons Millésime 1999**

EXPERT *Essential* At the top of the impressive Mailly range, this glorious concentrated Pinot Noir-dominated blend has an intense golden color and seductive richness but also a long life ahead if you cellar it further. Like most of the Mailly range, it is three parts Pinot Noir to one part Chardonnay and comes from some of the co-op's

» The influence of oak

Most champagne houses used to ferment their wines in oak barrels, but outside traditional producers such as Alfred Gratien, Bollinger, and Krug, this method declined in the 1950s and 1960s. Stainless steel became the norm; however, there is a trend among smaller quality houses and a new generation of growers to return to oak, particularly for the initial fermentation (some also partly age their wines in oak before bottling).

Fermentation in oak doesn't necessarily result in overtly oaky champagnes as most producers use old barrels that don't impart woody flavors to the wines and many use large *foudres* of 440 gallons or more capacity, where the ratio of wood to wine is very low.

The attraction of oak is the contact with the air, or what is known as micro-oxygenation. If the wine has the structure and personality to handle it, this process helps bring out aromas and flavor, adding complexity. It also has a beneficial effect of making the wine less prone to oxidation.

best and oldest vineyard parcels. It is a wine of considerable complexity.

» Exception Blanche Millésime 1999

A real rarity, this is a special vintage Blanc de Blancs style that combines Mailly Chardonnay with that from another cooperative (Les Viticulteurs d'Avize) based in Avize. The richness and fullness of Mailly Chardonnay blends with the power and intensity of Avize grapes to produce a penetrating and vivid wine that has a floral and citrus element and at this stage only a suggestion of the complexity that maturity will bring. It needs lavish food such as crayfish or lobster to show at its best.

Coteaux Champenois

A very small volume of still wine is produced in Champagne under the Coteaux Champenois appellation, most of it red. It is hard to buy outside the region and is typically produced by small growers based in *crus* such as Bouzy, Ay, Ambonnay, and Cumières, where mostly black grapes are planted. At their best in warm years, when black grapes get notably ripe, the wines tend to be like very light, fruity Burgundies, though critics say they are nearly always thin and acidic, which demonstrates why Champagne became a region specializing in sparkling wine, not table wine.

Vallée de la Marne

Beaumont des Crayères

64, Rue de la Liberté, 51530 Mardeuil

Tel: +33 (0)3 26 55 29 40

www.champagne-beaumont.com

The Beaumont des Crayères brand is produced by a medium-sized co-op located in the village of Mardeuil on the north side of the Vallée de la Marne, where most of the two hundred-odd growers are part-timers who tend the vines (on over five hundred acres) on weekends or during vacation. It is a characterful range that hits a high point with Nostalgie vintage, a classy act at a very good price.

» ### Grande Réserve Brut NV

A high percentage of Pinot Meunier in this blend accentuates the red-berry fruit flavors and helps make it an enjoyably forward, supplely mellow wine with a nutty note on the finish.

» ### Fleur Noir 2003 Brut Vintage

A Blanc de Noirs made from the super-ripe precocious 2003 harvest, which is a blend of 70 percent Pinot Noir and 30 percent Pinot Meunier. Exuberantly fruity with some very attractive red-berry juiciness and refreshing acidity, it is creamy-textured and seductive, a real charmer.

» ### Nostalgie Brut Vintage 1999

EXPERT *Essential* The co-op's top-of-the-range cuvée is a 65/35 Chardonnay-Pinot Noir blend of impressive length and quality that is described by the cognoscenti as a "mini-Krug," with quince-like fruit and a buttery, savory, toasty palate. In the glass it just gets better and better as it opens up.

Pannier

23, Rue Roger-Catillon, 02407 Château-Thierry

Tel: +33 (0)3 23 69 51 30
www.champagnepannier.com

Champagne Pannier was founded by Louis Eugène Pannier in 1899, in the village Dizy, adjacent to Épernay. In 1937, his son purchased medieval cellars in Château-Thierry, in the Marne Valley, and transferred his thriving champagne business there. The brand and the business were bought by a group of wine growers (COVAMA) in 1974, and this co-op now processes enough grapes to vinify more than four million bottles. COVAMA, which is part of Alliance Champagne, is also involved in the production of the Jacquart brand.

» ### Égérie de Pannier Rosé de Saignée Brut NV

EXPERT Essential A very pretty pale pink, this champagne has a lovely, perfumed floral nose with hints of fresh raspberries, while in the mouth it is delicate, poised, and beautifully balanced with a creamy mouthfeel. This is a hugely enjoyable and classy pink fizz, delicate yet intense.

» ### Égérie de Pannier Extra Brut Vintage 2000

The rich golden color suggests a ripeness that is delivered, with stone-fruit aromas and a full, soft, luscious texture, plus some savory mocha notes.

Words from the wise

Mark Jenner Bar Manager,
Coburg Bar, London, UK

» A champagne experience

Champagne evokes a perfect balance between mystery and wonder that has bewitched successive generations. It should be treated with a lightness of touch and a reverence saved for the oldest and rarest of liquids.

Glassware is paramount. I opt for two styles of Riedel glass: the Cuvée Prestige for most non-vintage and, for something that has a little more age to it, the Sauvignon Blanc to really bring out its full potential of expressions, to release the plethora of different aromas.

Sourcing and storage are key, especially in rare vintage cases. Provenance must be traceable right back to the maison itself, as many top wines are traded like commodities and could have traveled the globe. Dedicated EuroCave wine storage systems are the best type of storage, set at a consistent temperature between 44–46°F, mirroring the caves in which these wines were born.

Côte des Blancs

Nicolas Feuillatte CVC

Chouilly, 51206 Épernay

Tel: +33 (0)3 26 59 55 50 www.feuillatte.com

The Feuillatte brand is produced by the largest cooperative group in Champagne, based in Chouilly. Its forty-nine hundred members together own nearly one-fifth (over fourteen thousand acres) of the appellation's vineyards, which gives winemaker Jean-Pierre Vincent a huge palate of blending options to experiment with. With access to thirteen of Champagne's seventeen *grand cru* vineyards, he has made some very fine single-*cru* wines, and this range has now evolved into Grand Cru Pinot Noir and Grand Cru Chardonnay. There are also two oak-aged styles under the Cuvée 225 label. While the main nonvintage brand has become one of the top-five-selling champagnes worldwide, the most exciting wines are these niche products, often produced in relatively small quantities.

» **Cuvée Palmes d'Or 1999**

EXPERT *Essential* This vintage is quite a contrast to the lusher, full-bodied 1998 wine that preceded it, with more elegance and a noticeable chalky minerality on the palate. It is a 50/50

Pinot Noir-Chardonnay blend; the latter is a combination of fine citrus Chardonnays from the *grands crus* Côtes de Blancs villages of Chouilly, Cramant, and Le Mesnil-sur-Oger contrasted with the rich, ripe tropical fruit notes of Chardonnay from Montgueux, which adds a perceptible power and fatness.

>> **Cuvée 225 Vintage Rosé 2004**
A blend of equal proportions of Chardonnay and Pinot Noir with between 15 and 20 percent of red wine added for color, creating a fine coppery pink. This strawberry-fruited rosé is a new addition to the range to complement the white Cuvée 225, and like that wine it is all barrel-fermented in oak. But while this is a quite weighty, distinctive, savory style with some vanilla notes, it is not overtly oaky, nor heavy, as the component *crus* in the blend can handle this treatment.

Le Mesnil Cooperative

58, Grande-Rue, 51190 Le Mesnil-sur-Oger

Tel:+33 (0)3 26 57 53 23
www.champagnelemesnil.com

Based in the heart of the *grand cru* village of Le Mesnil-sur-Oger, this cooperative has around five hundred members who between them own some 754 acres of vineyards. The co-op mainly supplies the major *négociant* houses with top-quality still wines (*vins clairs*) for their brands. It also makes some wine, however, and its top cuvée, Sublime, lives up to its name; as the rereleased 1988 vintage shows, it can also age fantastically well.

» **Le Mesnil Brut Vintage 2004**

This still-youthful, all-Chardonnay fizz from the forward 2004 vintage is a slightly more generous, fuller style than some Blanc de Blancs champagnes, though it doesn't lack edge or concentration and will develop increasingly greater complexity over time.

Union Champagne

7, Rue Pasteur, 51190 Avize

Tel: +33 (0)3 26 57 94 22
www.union-champagne.fr

The eighteen hundred members of this cooperative between them have the largest group holdings of *grand* (1,976 acres) and *premier crus* (988 acres) in the Côte des Blancs. Much of the produce is sold on to the large houses for use in their top cuvées, but under its own De Saint Gall label, this co-op makes a consistently good range of Blanc de Blancs champagnes.

» **Cuvée Orpale Blanc de Blancs 1998**

EXPERT *Essential* The co-op's top wine is a fine blend of arguably the four best *grands crus* villages in the Côte des Blancs: Avize, Cramant, Oger, and Le Mesnil-sur-Oger. Pure, mineral with a distinctive and penetrating citrusy note, this is a long-keeper of considerable class and a fine example of the style.

» Possess

Buying retail

If you're looking to buy a specific bottle or are interested in buying to lay down for a few years, it is best to consult the seller or an expert first to find out which wines are likely to develop further, and when you might expect them to reach their peaks. You may have to search a little harder for specific and vintage champagnes, but there are good retailers around the world, and most will have websites as well.

UNITED STATES

Astor Wines
399 Lafayette Street, New York, NY 10003 USA
Tel: 212 674 7500 www.astorwines.com

Chambers Sreet Wines
148 Chambers Street, New York, NY 10007 USA
Tel: 212 227 1434 www.chambersstwines.com

Crush Wine
153 East Fifty-seventh Street, New York, NY 10022 USA
Tel: 212 980 9463 www.crushwineco.com

Le Dû's Wines
600 Washington Street, New York, NY 10014 USA
Tel: 212 924 6999 www.leduwines.com

Wine Library
586 Morris Avenue, Springfield, NJ 07081 USA
Tel: 973 376 0005 www.winelibrary.com

Flickinger Fine Wines
1222 Washington Court, Unit 201, Wilmette, IL 60091 USA Tel: 847 920 5046 www.flickingerwines.com

Fine Wine Brokers
4621 North Lincoln Avenue, Chicago, IL 60625 USA
Tel: 773 989 8166 www.fwbchicago.com

Perman Wine Selections
802 West Washington Boulevard, Chicago, IL 60607
USA Tel: 312 666 4417 www.permanwine.com

Vinopolis Wine Shop
1025 Southwest Washington Street, Portland, OR 97205
USA Tel: 503 223 6002 www.vinopoliswineshop.com

K&L Wines
3005 El Camino Real, Redwood City, CA 94061 USA
Tel: 650 364 8544 www.klwines.com

Twenty Twenty Wine Merchants
2020 Cotner Avenue, Los Angeles, CA 90025 USA
Tel: 310 447 2020 www.2020wines.com

Wine House
2311 Cotner Avenue, Los Angeles, CA 90064 USA
Tel: 310 479 3731 www.winehouse.com

EUROPE

C Comme Champagne
8, Rue Gambetta, 51200 Épernay, France
Tel: +33 (0)3 26 32 09 55 www.c-comme.fr

La Vinocave
43, Place Drouet d'Erlon, 51100 Reims, France
Tel: +33 (0)3 26 40 60 07

Les Caves du Forum
10, Rue Courmaux, 51100 Reims, France
Tel: +33 (0)3 26 79 15 15 www.lescavesduforum.com

Entrepot du Vin, Berlin
Fasanenstr. 42, D-10719 Berlin, Germany
Tel. +49 (0)30 88551727 www.entrepot-du-vin.de

Jeroboams, Belgravia
50–52 Elizabeth Street, London SW1W 9PB UK
Tel: +44 (0)207 730 8108 www.jeroboams.co.uk

WEBSITES
www.champagnewines.com
www.farrvintners.com
www.thewinesociety.com
www.justchampagne.co.uk

Rare and collectible items

There isn't much of a market for rare, old vintages of champagne, certainly not one as developed as that for the top wines from Bordeaux. If you are buying as an investment, you should go for complete cases of the most sought-after champagnes from the top vintages. Magnums are more collectable than bottles and tend to fetch proportionately higher prices.

Champagne investments

Three prestige brands dominate the vintage market at the top end: Louis Roederer Cristal, which regularly commands the highest prices; vintage Krug in second place (although 1982 Krug tends to sell for more than 1982 Cristal); and Dom Pérignon, which is partly less valuable because it is produced in far greater volume.

The picture is complicated by the fact that all three brands have small volumes of library releases that are given extra aging and are periodically put on sale by the owners of the brands—Dom Pérignon, for example, usually has two of its Oenothéque releases in the market at any given time.

The rosé versions of Cristal and Dom Pérignon also fetch considerable premiums on their white equivalents. Krug has two single-vineyard wines in Clos du Mesnil and Clos d'Ambonnay, the latter being one of the most collectable champagnes of recent times, especially its initial 1995 vintage.

Prices for other prestige cuvées by top houses can also be high, especially for mature vintages. Veuve

Clicquot's La Grande Dame, Taittinger's Comte de Champagne, Dom Ruinart, and Pol Roger's Sir Winston Churchill Cuvée also have a following. The 1990 Pol recently fetched more than La Grande Dame and Dom Pérignon at auction.

Personal consumption

If you are looking to buy top vintage champagne to lay down for your own future consumption, far better value is to be found with the straight vintage wines of the top houses: the prices of older champagnes are certainly not astronomic compared with top older vintages from Bordeaux and Burgundy.

The top vintages to go for over the past three decades are 2006, 2002, 1999, 1996, 1995, 1990, 1989, 1988, and 1985. There are also some very good 1998 and 1999 releases; top-class 1982s and 1983s if you can find them; and Krug 1981 is seen by the Krug family as one of their best vintages of the twentieth century. In the seventies, 1979 and 1975 stand out, while there were five greats in the sixties: 1969, 1966, 1964, 1962, and 1961, with the latter being the star, like in Bordeaux.

Where to buy

Buying at auction is one of the best options for finding rare bottles, though this market tends to be restricted to the prestige cuvées, except for a few online auction sites. Two of the best international auction houses are Sotheby's (www.sothebys.com) and Christie's (www.christies.com). Otherwise, high-end wine merchants sometimes have a good range of older champagnes.

Champagne storage

To store champagne you need a dark, cool place, free of smells and vibration, where the temperature fluctuates very little. Humidity is also important: if it is too dry, the corks tend to dry out and cease being an effective seal. The ideal temperature is probably between 50 and 60°F, perhaps toward the lower end of this scale for champagne, as the cellar temperatures in the caves of Reims and Épernay are generally somewhere between 52 and 54°F. The deep cellars at Pol Roger are slightly colder than most in Champagne, at around 49°F, and some see this as a significant fact in making particularly long-lived wines. Certainly the lower the temperature (within the 50 to 60°F parameter) the more slowly the champagne will evolve, and while no real harm will come to champagne stored at slightly above 60°F, so long as there are not significant fluctuations in temperature, it will develop more rapidly.

If you don't have suitable cellar space in your home you can purchase a special, humidity-controlled wine fridge, though even the largest of these can store only a few dozen bottles. The alternative is to pay for professional storage at a reputable wine merchant that offers this service, which is likely to cost a couple of dollars per case per month. This could be a good solution if you have large amounts of young wine, but it does restrict your ability to open a bottle at will.

Serving and etiquette

One of the leading competitions for sommeliers requires participants to pour equal amounts of champagne from a magnum into twelve glasses, without going back to top any up, avoiding spillage and without pausing while filling a glass, even if it looks like it will overflow. For mere mortals, who may struggle to get the cork out at all, here are some simple guidelines to follow.

Finding the right temperature

To serve, you need a lower temperature than for storage, ideally between 43 and 50°F (towards the higher end for the best mature wines) as this should allow the slow release of the mousse. Too warm and the bottle may be dangerous to open and, once it is, the fizz will be quickly lost. The most efficient way to chill a bottle is in an ice bucket filled with water, plus a big handful of ice cubes, for between ten and fifteen minutes. A couple of hours in the door of a fridge should also be about right, but if you leave it longer than a day, the cork tends to stick, making opening the bottle more difficult.

Opening a bottle

Remove the wire cage that holds the cork in place, being careful to keep your hand over the cork as you do so, to stop it from flying out. Then hold the bottle at a forty-five-degree angle (take care not to point it at anyone), grip the cork firmly in one hand and, holding the base of the bottle in the other, gradually turn the bottle, not the cork. Once you feel the cork starting to move, hold it down so it comes out slowly "with a whisper" not a loud pop. Make sure you have a couple of glasses in front of you, just in case the cork does come out faster than you intended. Champagne is too expensive to spill on the floor.

Pouring champagne

It is better to put a little wine in each glass first and then go back and top up each one. You can normally fill six or seven appropriate glasses from a single bottle, leaving room in the glass for it to breathe. Use clean glasses—detergent is the enemy of bubbles. The secret is to rinse glasses a couple of times in hot water after washing.

Glassware

Flutes are better than the open flat coupe to preserve the bubbles and capture the wine's aroma—the broad surface of the coupe glass means the bubbles will disappear more quickly. Flutes that are in the tulip shape are the best, certainly from a tasting point of view. For older vintage champagnes and prestige cuvées, a fine white wine glass is a good alternative.

Champagne and food

It is not an accident that most champagne in restaurants is consumed as an aperitif; it is a great appetite stimulator. But it also works very well with a surprisingly large range of foods.

Combine lighter styles with canapés and cocktail nibbles, cashew nuts, or perhaps a brunch of smoked salmon and scrambled eggs. Fresh and lightly cooked seafood (oysters and scallops for example) can be paired with a young fresh Blanc de Blancs. In restaurants in Paris and Reims, the minerality of some extra brut and *nondosé* cuvées is often matched with shellfish to good effect, as well as sushi and sashimi dishes.

Champagne also has a natural affinity with luxury ingredients, such as caviar, lobster, and *foie gras*. It is a good foil for the saltiness of caviar, although lobster probably needs a richer, aged style of Blanc de Blanc, and *foie gras*, a good-quality sweet style or mature old vintage champagne.

For meaty dishes, such as pigeon or other game birds, roast duck, or even rare lamb cutlets, aged vintage rosé majoring on Pinot Noir can be delicious. The toasty richness of great mature champagne from a vintage such as a 1988 is mind-blowing with roast turbot or Bresse chicken stuffed with truffles. And finally, if you want to end a meal with fine champagne, it goes well with all sorts of cheese but particularly with hard varieties, such as Beaufort, Parmesan, or extra-aged Cantal.

Champagne cocktails

While some people may argue against mixing champagne, there's no doubt that a champagne cocktail can be an impressive creation. The classic champagne cocktail is an old favorite; the others are particularly fine modern creations. All of these should be served in a champagne flute.

Classic Champagne Cocktail

1 fl. oz. cognac

Brown sugar cube

4 drops of angostura bitters

4 fl. oz. champagne

Carefully drip the angostura bitters onto the sugar cube. Pour the cognac into a flute, add the soaked sugar cube, and top up with champagne.

Blushing Bubbles

2 tsp. passion fruit purée

1 tbsp. raspberry purée

4 fl. oz. champagne

Mix together the chilled purées and pour into flute. Top up with champagne slowly and carefully (as it tends to fizz up and overflow). Mix with a long-handled spoon.

Words from the wise

Xavier Rousset
Master Sommelier, Texture
Champagne Bar, London, UK

» Matching champagne with food

When matching food with champagne, *non dosé* and extra brut styles work well with lighter dishes, while with a butter-based sauce, a higher-dosage style is preferable. For a seafood dish, match the wine to the richness of the sauce. Try contrasting a wild mushroom risotto with a Blanc de Noirs, ideally a mature vintage style. Less fizziness with greater age means more mouth texture to the champagne, making it ideal for this sort of earthy, creamy dish.

For nonvintage, consider the blend first: a Chardonnay-led style needs freshness and acidity in the dish, whereas Pinot-dominant cuvées work well with spicier and more earthy ingredients. With vintage champagne, contrast the power of the dish with the blend and style of the specific year. I'd choose very different food drinking a 1996, with its marked acidity, than I would to match the ripeness of 1989. Made mostly in a crisp, light, and (sometimes) fruity style, nonvintage rosé makes the ideal aperitif.

French 75

| 0.5 fl. oz. premium gin |
| 1 tsp. freshly squeezed lemon juice |
| 1 tsp. simple syrup |
| 4 fl. oz. champagne |

Combine the gin, lemon, and syrup and shake well. Pour into a flute and top up with champagne.

Luxury Mojito

| 2 fl. oz. three-year-old rum |
| 4–5 slices of fresh lime |
| Handful of fresh mint leaves |
| Brown sugar |
| 1.5 fl. oz. champagne |

Muddle the lime, mint, and sugar in a pestle and mortar until well mixed, then add the rum. Add crushed ice, strain into a flute, and top up with champagne.

La Vie en Rose

| 1 sugar cube |
| 2 dashes Peychaud's Bitters |
| ½ fl. oz. St. Germain (or any elderflower liqueur) |
| Champagne |

Drop a sugar cube into the bottom of a champagne flute. Hit it with two dashes of bitters, and then add the liqueur. Fill the rest of the flute with a dry, nonvintage champagne. Garnish with an orchid petal or small edible flower.

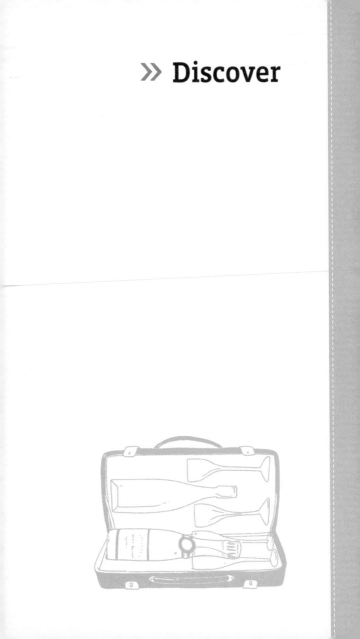

» Discover

Champagne bars

There are many bars and restaurants around the world that stock a good range of champagnes. To help you find particularly impressive examples, below is a selection of those that are worth hunting out, whether it is for their range, rare vintages, great value, or, in the best, a combination of all three.

UNITED STATES

The Bubble Lounge New York 228 West Broadway, New York, NY 10013 Tel: 212 431 3433 www.bubblelounge.com

Champagne Bar The Plaza New York, 768 Fifth Avenue, New York, NY 10019 Tel: 212 759 3000 www.theplaza.com/dining/champagne-bar/

Corkbuzz Wine Studio 13 East Thirteenth Street, New York, NY 10003 Tel: 647 873 6071 www.corkbuzz.com

Del Posto 85 Tenth Avenue, New York, NY 10011 Tel: 212 497 8090 www.delposto.com

Flûte Midtown 205 West Fifty-fourth Street, New York, NY 10019 Tel: 212 265 5169 www.flutebar.com

Terroir 413 East Twelfth Street, New York, NY 10009 Tel: 646 602 1300 www.wineisterroir.com

RumBa Rum & Champagne Bar 510 Atlantic Avenue, Boston, MA 02210 Tel: 617 747 1000

Metropolitan Room at the Napoleon Bistro 1847 Columbia Road NW, Washington, DC 20009 Tel: 202 299 9630 www.napoleondc.com

Pops for Champagne 601 North State Street, Chicago, IL 60611, Tel: 312 266 7677 www.popsforchampagne.com

Corridor 44 1433 Larimer Street, Denver, CO 80202 Tel: 303 893 0044 www.corridor44.com

Laguna Champagne Bar The Palazzo, 3325 Las Vegas Boulevard South, Las Vegas, NV 89109 Tel: 702 607 7777 www.palazzo.com

Ambonnay 107 Southeast Washington Street, Portland, OR 97214 Tel: 503 575 4861 www.ambonnaybar.com

Pix Patisserie 2225 East Burnside Street, Portland, OR 97214 Tel: 971 271 7166 www.pixpatisserie.com

The Bubble Lounge San Francisco 714 Montgomery Street, San Francisco, CA 94111 Tel: 415 434 4204 www.bubblelounge.com

Sigh 29 East Napa Street, Sonoma, CA 95476 Tel: 707 996 2444 www.sighsonoma.com

EUROPE

Le Bar 228 Le Meurice, 228, Rue de Rivoli, 75001 Paris Tel: +33 (0)1 44 58 10 10 www.lemeurice.com

Flûte l'Etoile 19 Rue de l'Etoile, 75017 Paris Tel: +33 (0)1 45 72 10 14 www.flutebar.com

Bar München Maximilianstrasse 36, 80539 Munich Tel: +49 (0)89 22 90 90 www.barmuenchen.com

Hotel Louis C Jacob Elbchaussee 401–403, 22609 Hamburg Tel: +49 (0)40 82 25 50 www.hotel-jacob.de

Ritz Carlton Potsdamer Platz 3, 10785 Berlin Tel: +49 (0)30 33 77 77 www.ritzcarlton.com

Rutz Weinbar Chausseestraße 8, 10115 Berlin Tel: +49 (0)30 24 62 87 60 www.rutz-weinbar.de

Bubbles Champagne Bar Sadovaya Triumfalnaya Street, 10/13, Building 1, Moscow Tel: +7 495 694 6987

Kalina Bar Novinsky Boulevard, No 8, Building Lotte Plaza, 21st floor, Moscow Tel: +7 495 229 5519 www.kalinabar.ru

Texture Restaurant & Champagne Bar 34 Portman Street, London W1H 7BY Tel: +44 (0)207 224 0028 www.texture-restaurant.co.uk

St Pancras Champagne Bar St Pancras Station, Pancras Road, Camden Town, London NW1 2QP Tel: +44 (0)207 843 7688 www.searcys.co.uk

Amuse Bouche 51 Parsons Green Lane, Fulham, London SW6 4JA Tel: +44 (0)207 371 8517 www.abcb.co.uk

Épernay Wine Bar The Electric Press Building, 12 Great George Street, Leeds LS1 3DW Tel: +44 (0)113 242 9977 www.epernaychampagnebars.com

Champagne travel

To find champagne worthy of the name and experience all the region has to offer, you have to go there. Only in Champagne can you source stock at the major houses, brought up from their own deep, cool chalk cellars where all the wine matures in perfect conditions.

The three main centers of Reims, Épernay, and Troyes have plenty to offer the wine-loving visitor. In Reims and Épernay there are impressive tours of some of the major houses' spectacular cellars. All three towns offer visitors the chance to buy unusual cuvées, growers' champagnes, and older vintages not usually seen outside France, plus there are plenty of high-quality restaurants.

Cellar tours

While in the region you'll probably want to visit a cellar or two. The Romans originally dug out these *crayères* in their search for building materials, carving out great blocks of chalk that amazingly were hauled out of the narrow necks to the pits by ropes. The oldest cellars still run in line to the southern side of Reims, grouped around the Place du Général Gouraud, and this is where you will find the houses of Pommery, Taittinger, Veuve Clicquot, and Ruinart. On the other side of the city, GH Mumm has a cellar tour that's well worth trying.

The most spectacular cellars to visit are arguably at Pommery, where once you have climbed down the 116 steps, you can clearly see the huge conical-shaped chalk pits that were excavated by the Romans. As a bonus, there are also dramatic giant carvings, made by Gustave Navlet in the 1880s, which are literally hewn out of the soft, chalky walls of the *crayères*. Ruinart also has an impressive cellar in Reims, with steps descending one hundred feet into the vast subterranean cathedral-like *crayères*.

GH Mumm
29, Rue du Champ de Mars, 51053 Reims
Tel: +33 (0)3 26 49 59 69 www.mumm.com

Pommery
5, Place du Général Gouraud, 51689 Reims
Tel: +33 (0)3 26 61 62 63 www.pommery.com

Ruinart
4, Rue des Crayères, 51100 Reims
Tel: +33 (0)3 26 77 51 51 www.ruinart.com

Taittinger
9, Place Saint-Nicaise, 51100 Reims
Tel: +33 (0)3 26 85 43 35 www.taittinger.com

Vineyards

While visiting the major houses dotted around the city, you'll find some wines that are not exported. To buy champagnes by growers, which if you find the right addresses offer some of the top wines and best deals in Champagne, you really have to leave the confines of the city and head out to the vineyards. You could easily visit several in a leisurely morning or afternoon tour, though ideally you should contact them in advance to check availability. Here you are buying wine directly from the people who make it. There is no better way of learning about champagne.

For something out of the ordinary, some growers organize special *jour de vendange* trips during the harvest, typically in mid-September, when you have the chance to pick and press grapes and also try the champagnes made by some small producers. Complete lists of wine growers, offering these grape-harvest days, are available from the Aube (Tel: +33 (0)3 25 42 50 00) and Marne Tourist Boards (Tel: +33 (0)3 26 68 37 52).

Further contacts

For more information on visiting the region, the following contacts are useful. The Le Comité interprofessionel du vin de Champagne (CIVC), listed below, also has thirteen offices outside France in champagne's main markets around the world.

CIVC
Épernay at 5, Rue Henri Martin, 51200 Épernay
Tel: +33 (0)3 26 51 19 30 www.champagne.fr

Reims tourist office
2, Rue Guillaume de Machault, 51100 Reims
Tel: +33 (0)8 92 70 13 51 www.reims-tourisme.com

Épernay tourist office
7, Avenue de Champagne, 512011 Épernay
Tel: +33 (0)3 26 53 33 00 www.ot-epernay.fr

Troyes tourist office
16, Boulevard Carnot, 10000 Troyes
Tel: +33 (0)3 25 82 62 70
www.tourisme-troyes.com

Syndicat Général des Vignerons
Les Champagnes de Vignerons, 17–19 Avenue de Champagne, 51205 Épernay, Tel: +33 (0)3 26 59 55 00
www.champagnesdevignerons.com

Glossary

Assemblage Putting together a blend of different wines and/or years.

Autolysis A bi-chemical process during which yeast cells are broken down.

Barrique A small oak barrel of about 50 gallons, as typically used in Bordeaux and Burgundy respectively.

Bottle-age The amount of time a wine spends in bottle before it is consumed; such ageing has a mellowing effect.

Chef de cave Literally, the cellarmaster, who is typically the winemaker, or chief blender.

Cooperative-manipulante (CM) A co-operative making and selling champagne.

Crémant A gently sparkling wine with around 3.5 atmospheres of pressure. Since 1994 the name is no longer allowed in Champagne, although a few producers still make such wines. It is kept for sparkling wines from other parts of France.

Cru Literally "growth," as in *premier cru* (first growth). It refers to a specific commune or village.

Cuvée The juice from the first and best pressing of the grapes. It also refers to a specific champagne blend.

Crayère A Gallo-Roman chalk pit dug out for building materials, now used as cellars.

Dégorgement Disgorging—the removal of the deposit that forms in a champagne bottle after the secondary fermentation is complete.

Demi-muid A large wooden barrel, mostly made of oak, of around 130 gallons capacity.

Échelle des crus Literally "ladder of growths," this is a percentile rating scale by which all 319 *crus* are assessed.

Foudre A large wooden cask.

Grand(s) cru(s) The best vineyards, all rated 100 percent on the *échelle des crus*.

Gyropalette A computerized riddling (*remuage*) system in a metal cube-shaped container, typically holding five hundred bottles.

Lees A sediment typically made from dead yeast cells that fall to the bottom of the barrel or tank in the winemaking process.

Liqueur de dosage The sugar levels added to a bottle of champagne when it is disgorged (expressed in grams of sugar per liter). It is typically made from mature wine and sugar.

Liqueur de tirage A liqueur added to the still wine to create the secondary fermentation in the bottle.

Marc Term for a single pressing of grapes; 8,800 lbs is the amount that is processed in a traditional basket press.

Méthode traditionelle The classic way of making sparkling wine where the secondary fermentation that creates the bubbles takes place in the bottle as opposed to the tank method, in which carbon dioxide is added to the wine.

Monocru Champagne from a single *cru* or village.

Mousse The stream of bubbles in a glass of sparkling wine.

Mousseux Fully sparkling wine with 5 to 6 atmospheres of pressure.

Négociant-manipulant (NM) Champagne merchant who may buy grapes or wines from others to blend their wines.

NV Nonvintage.

Pièce A small oak barrel, usually 45 gallons in Champagne.

Premier(s) cru(s) A village or commune rated 90–99 percent on the *échelle des crus*.

Prise de mousse The creation of the mousse by the secondary fermentation in bottle.

Pupitres Wooden containers with holes in them into which the bottles of champagne fit for the *remuage* process.

Récoltant-manipulant (RM) A grower making champagne from his/her own grapes, although growers are permitted to buy or swap with another grower up to 5 percent of their harvest.

Remuage (riddling) The process of turning, twisting, shaking, and gradually tilting bottles to encourage the sediment deposit to gradually settle in the neck of the bottle on the crown cap or cork.

Saignée A method of making rosé, in which pigment is bled from the grape skins.

Reserve wines Older wines from previous harvests kept back for blending purposes.

Taille The juice from the second or third pressing of grapes and thus inferior.

Vendange Harvest.

Vigneron A wine grower.

Vins clairs The term used for still wines that have gone through their first but not secondary fermentation.

Index

143

144